Rousing the Sleeping Giant

...A powerful tale of mindfulness for life

Suenita S. Maharaj

ROUSING THE SLEEPING GIANT
Copyright © 2017 by Suenita S. Maharaj

All rights reserved. No part of this publication may be reproduced, distributed, or transmitted in any form or by any means, including photocopying, recording, or other electronic or mechanical methods, without the prior written permission of the author, except in the case of brief quotations embodied in critical reviews and certain other non-commercial uses permitted by copyright law.

Printed and bound in Canada at McNally Robinson Booksellers. 1120 Grant Avenue, Winnipeg, Manitoba R3M 2A6

Cover designed by McNally Robinson Self-Publishing
www.mcnallyrobinson.com/selfpublishing
Cover art by Suenita Maharaj
Suenitamaharaj.com

First Edition
ISBN: 978-1-77280-108-8

Editing by Final Copy Editorial Services

Dedication

To my daughters: Anjali, Antara, and Anaka
My princess, my angel, my fairy
My inspiration for writing this book

"Everything is created twice, first in the mind and then in reality."

Robin Sharma

Rousing
the Sleeping Giant

Suenita S. Maharaj, M.Ed.

Table of Contents

Dedication
Table of Contents
Introduction

Chapter 1 2
Meet Pavlov's Dog
"Life is what happens while you're busy making plans"

Chapter 2 30
Switching from Autopilot to Manual
Your thoughts can fuel your success or feed your failure

Chapter 3 40
Ryan in Wonderland
"The mind is a wonderful servant, but a terrible master"

Chapter 4 62
Change Your Thoughts Change Your Reality
A minute of clarity is a minute of prosperity

Chapter 5 72
Who Hijacked My Emotions?
Claim your power to choose your reaction

Chapter 6 88
Divine Play
"Our own worst enemy cannot harm us as much as unwise thoughts"

Chapter 7 98
Thoughts are Just Thoughts. Thoughts are not Facts
"Today is the first day of the rest of your life" Live it !

Introduction

In the story that follows you will come to understand that your thoughts can fuel your success or feed your failure. This book comprises some of what I have learned from my study of ancient Vedanta and Buddhist philosophies over the past 20 years, combined with cutting-edge research in neuroscience and social psychology.

The secrets you learn will move you from living on autopilot to making conscious decisions that will help you stay grounded in the present moment and live the life you choose, rather than becoming tangled in the mediocrity and daily drudgery of habitual living. In short, it will open the door to a degree of control you never knew you had.

The story itself is based on the life experiences of many successful people who have moved themselves from the depths of unfulfilled, hectic, fast-paced living to contented, joyful living of each day as they choose.

Walk in the footsteps of one such person, Ryan, and experience his daily life in a high-stress work world with an unfulfilling marriage, and a daughter he has disappointed time and time again. Forced to acknowledge how he has contributed to his own stress and unhappiness, he enters an unusual work world of chimpanzees, life-size images of himself and home movies. His journey will change the way you think about your relationships, your emotions, and your behaviours.

No matter what you may want to change in your life, no matter what your circumstances are, these secrets will help you if you apply them to your daily living. Let today be the beginning of your journey toward changing your life forever, at work, in play, with family, friends and lovers.

Suenita S. Maharaj, M.Ed.

Chapter 1

Meet Pavlov's Dog

"Life is what happens while you're busy making other plans."
Allen Saunders

It was a beautiful spring afternoon. The sun was shifting its gaze from behind the clouds, birds were chirping, and a light breeze was in the air. Ryan was oblivious to the beauty surrounding him as he ran into the Discovery Centre. He was breathing heavily as he looked at the time on his cell phone. He quickened his pace to the front counter where he was greeted by a woman with auburn hair, wearing a crisp white shirt and black pants. She smiled at Ryan as he approached.

"Hi," she said. "My name is Mila. Can I help you?"

She was much too cheerful for Ryan's liking. "Yes," he puffed. "Where… where is the Negotiating With Yourself Program?"

"It's just down the hall and to the right," Mila replied, pointing to a long hallway with white walls. "Would you like a glass of water?"

"No, no, I'm going to be late as it is if I don't go now," he said, annoyed by her question.

But Mila, recognizing his agitated state, calmly repeated her directions while, again, motioning with her hand. "Down the hall and to your right."

"But there are two hallways," Ryan replied, rolling his eyes in wonder that she apparently did not know that.

Mila, used to people displaying such frantic behaviour, simply motioned once more to the hallway now immediately in front of Ryan. "Straight ahead," she said.

Ryan's irritation deepened the furrows in his forehead. Although he was only 39, he looked 10 years older than that. The long work days had taken their toll, not just on his physical health but also on his marriage and his relationship with his 10-year-old daughter, Tara.

As he moved up the career ladder he found himself growing more and more distant from his wife, Leela. The Friday nights with her at their favourite restaurant were replaced with networking meetings. When he did happen to have a free Friday, she often had already made other plans, having expected him to be busy at work.

He quickly marched down the hall, glad to be rid of Mila and her time-wasting cheerfulness. Another glance at his cell phone told him it is 8:28. "Perfect, a couple of minutes to spare," he mumbled to himself.

At the end of the hallway, he opened the door to his immediate right to enter a circular room with bare white walls. It was an odd setup, one Ryan had never seen before. On the periphery were four doors, each with a sign of some sort hanging from the door handle. In the middle of the room were two white leather chairs and a glass coffee table with a white box on it, along with a glass bowl of apples and pears.

Ryan looked at each of the doors with curiosity but could not see the writing on the signs from where he stood, which reminds him that he has been having trouble seeing at a distance. *'Got to get to the optometrist,'* he thought to himself.

As he moved toward the door closest to him he was able to read the sign on it: "Today is the First Day of the Rest of Your Life". He moved to the next door: "Monkey Mind". The sign on the third door said "Who Hijacked My Emotions" and as he moved to the final door, he shook his head in surprise. The sign on it said, "Ryan in Wonderland".

"Hi again!" Mila's voice startled him from his thoughts. He turned to her with a "What now? look in his eyes.

"You were in such a rush I didn't get a chance to give you your orientation sheet," she said.

"It's already 8:35," he replied with annoyance. "Wasn't this supposed to start at 8:30?"

"Oh, but it has started," Mila replied with a comforting smile. "Here you go," she added, handing him a sheet of paper with three numbered sentences on it. "Bye now. Enjoy your day, Ryan."

Ryan sunk into one of the white leather chairs and started reading what was on the sheet of paper she had given him:

1) **Please place your cell phone in the white box on the table, lock the box and keep the key. You can get it on your way out.**

"Is this a joke? No way!" he said, raising his voice. The more he read, the more annoyed he became.

2) **When you put your phone in the white box, take out the electronic bracelet from the box and put it on your wrist.**

3) **The first 15 minutes of each day will be spent in quiet solitude. Please clear your mind of any thoughts having to do with the past, or future. Focus on creating space in your mind for the afternoon ahead.**

"Electronic bracelet?" he snickered. "What the heck is this? Shock therapy?"

Already angry at the thought of having to take training while work is piling up back at the office, his mind began barking frantic thoughts at him, thoughts that made him upset and more frustrated.

'Why the hell do I have to be here? This is such BS. I don't need training, I need time... time, and maybe

they can try taking some projects off my plate. That's what would help me lead my team.'

Ryan had had his annual performance review just last month. His manager, Lance, told him at the time that he would benefit from the Negotiating With Yourself Program, particularly if he was planning to apply for an executive position that had recently been advertised. He felt certain that Lance didn't think he was qualified for the position and that annoyed Ryan. The suggestion that he go for more training made him feel all the more certain Lance was working against him.

In his defence, Ryan insisted he had already taken all the training available for his job and listed a few of the courses he had aced: project management, inclusive leadership, crisis intervention, budgeting, equity and diversity.

But his resistance had fallen on deaf ears. Lance insisted it would be like no other training he had ever experienced and would change his view of himself, his relationships, and his view of the world… and not just at work but also at home with family and friends… even with his daughter.

For his part, Lance was aware of the dissatisfaction Ryan felt with his family life. He knew that Ryan had recently missed one of Tara's dance recitals because he was working late, and through the thin office walls he would often hear Ryan arguing with Leela about his being late for picking Tara up from her after-school program.

As he sat waiting for someone to come and tell him what to do, Ryan's emotions shifted from aggravation at having to take the training at all, to anger at being made to wait. He glanced at the door he had come through but there was still no sign of anyone joining him so he took his phone from his pocket. Just as he started to reply to an email he was startled away from it by a woman's voice, which seemed to come from an intercom system.

"Please place your phone in the box on the table and place the bracelet on your wrist."

Ryan was convinced he was on one of those hidden camera shows. He stood up, tucked in his navy shirt, and scanned the room in search of the hidden camera.

"We will restart your 15 minutes of transition time as soon as you put your phone in the box," the intercom voice said. "But don't despair. We will add 15 minutes to your day so you don't miss any of the training. Please enjoy this quiet time to relax, and clear a space in your mind for the afternoon ahead."

The last thing Ryan felt like doing was relaxing. Instead, his frustration escalated at the thought of having to be there for an additional 15 minutes. He had his evening fully scheduled and was not about to change it. To begin with, he needed to pick up a prescription for his mother after work and an extra 15 minutes would mean getting caught in rush-hour traffic and throw everything off. He probably wouldn't make it home in time for supper.

Leela liked to keep Tara on a schedule for supper so she could have some play time before bed. Not to mention he needed to read an audit report before tomorrow morning's meeting.

Ryan's palms began to sweat at the thought of what having to stay an extra 15 minutes would mean. The idea of not having access to his phone made him angrier than even he expected.

"This has to be a joke," he said out loud." Where's the damn hidden camera?"

The intercom voice repeated the same message.

"We will restart your 15 minutes of transition time as soon as you put your phone in the box. Please enjoy this quiet time to relax, and clear a space in your mind for your afternoon."

Again, Ryan stood up abruptly and began to pace back and forth, frantic as to how he could possibly manage an entire afternoon without his cell phone. A list of possible calamities started to race through his mind. A client might reconsider hiring his firm and he would need to talk to them to put them at ease. The budget committee might need more information to be able to make a decision on his project submission. And Anaka, his new employee, might be spreading gossip about him being sexist. What if his VP got wind of that, and tried to reach him! On and on came a myriad of dreadful things that could go wrong.

Once again, his thoughts were interrupted by the voice on the intercom as if it, or someone, was reading his mind.

"You're signed out on the office white board as being in training, as well as on your electronic calendar, and your email messages give your administrative assistant's number in case of any urgent issues. That person will reach us and we will get the message to you."

Ryan was shocked and became more convinced that this had to be some kind of a hidden camera hoax. He finally decided to play along, at least for the next few minutes, and placed his cell phone in the white box. He locked it and put the key in his pocket. He knew that was a bad idea but was immediately surprised at just how incomplete he felt without it. The uneasiness was very disconcerting.

He picked up the bracelet, which looked more like a pulse-tracking device used for exercising, and placed it on his wrist.

"Thank you," said the voice from the intercom. "We have notification that your phone has been placed in the box. Please enjoy some transition time in preparation for your afternoon."

Ryan was not used to doing just one thing at a time. He was a master at multitasking and proud of it. He was the guy who could finish a spreadsheet while watching TV with Tara, respond to e-mails in between, and put in a load of laundry if necessary. He believed you should not do anything unless you can accomplish at least two things with one action. He never allowed himself to lose a spare minute, ever. In bank lines, he was the guy busily responding to his emails or booking his next dentist appointment. A moment that's lost is a moment that costs! That was his motto and he loved to chant it to his work team. At the end of every meeting he would say, "Remember people, a moment that's lost is a moment that costs."

He walked back to the leather chair and plopped down into it with a sigh of defeat. As he observed his surroundings, the white walls, the doors, the table in front of him, a more soothing sound came over the intercom.

"Now take this time to relax and clear a space in your mind for today's session."

Ryan found it difficult to stop the flood of thoughts about all the work that was piling up at the office and all of his personal deadlines. It was tax season and he had to file his and Leela's tax returns. And he still had to orient Anaka to the audit process.

As he went from one concern to another he became more and more anxious at the thought of each. It was a long frustrating 15 minutes but, once again, his thoughts were interrupted when the door opened unexpectedly and Lance entered.

"What the heck are you doing here?" he asked his boss. Lance was the last person Ryan expected, or wanted to see. He was still upset over Lance's implication that he was not ready for an executive position.

"Oh," Lance replied casually. "I'm taking a training program on managing difficult employees. You know my motto. You only stop learning when you're dead.... So have you had a chance to decide what room you'd like to enter today?"

"What room I would like to enter? Is that why those doors are there? Nobody told me what to do and, damn it, they made me lock my phone away in that box," he added while pointing to the white box on the table.

"Oh," Lance said, "me too. It's a rule here, and to tell you the truth, I'm kind of enjoying the time away from it. I feel like one of Pavlov's dogs when I have my cell phone on me."

"Whose dogs?"

"Pavlov's… He was a guy who did experiments with dogs in the 1890s. His experiments were based on the fact that whenever he came into the room to feed his dogs, they started to salivate, even though he hadn't given them any food yet. So basically, the dogs came to associate his coming into the room with getting food."

Lance paused for a moment then continued in response to Ryan's puzzled expression. "You see, they didn't even have to have food in front of them. They anticipated getting food and their bodies automatically reacted. So Pavlov decided to see if he could actually train them to salivate to the sound of a bell. He called it "anticipatory salivation," and it worked! After a few times of ringing the bell just before giving the dogs their food, they started to salivate at the sound of the bell, with no food present." He paused again, and then went on.

"That's why I turn the sound off on my phone unless I am expecting something I need right away. I don't want to be one of Pavlov's dogs."

"Well," Ryan responded, "I guess that's what they mean when they say it's a dog's life. You can salivate even without food." He laughed at his own joke but Lance didn't look impressed. He ignored the attempt at humour and continued speaking.

"Anyway, Ryan, I told them I would be coming by to see you and they told me to tell you that your 15 minutes was up you could pick a door for this afternoon's training session. Anyway, I have to get back to my own session. Enjoy your day." As he left the room Ryan approached the Monkey Mind door.

Monkey Mind

"Life is what happens to you while you're busy making other plans."

John Lennon (Beautiful Boy)

He bumped into a chair and stopped abruptly. He squinted and adjusted his vision from the bright light in the circular room to the dimmed lighting in the Monkey Mind room. As his eyes adjusted, he focused his gaze on the front of the room and a large stage with a backdrop that looked like a forest scene from a movie.

The trees were almond-brown and towering, with thick, lush green foliage. The ground was strewn with tan and green leaves, branches and twigs. A woody, organic smell prevailed, which Ryan recognized from his youthful hikes through the woods around their summer cottage. The sound of birds chirping and screeching filled the air. Clumps of moss at the base of the trees covered areas where roots protruded from the ground.

As his eyes became more accustomed to the light, Ryan cautiously approached. It was only then that he noticed the entire stage was enclosed in what looked like Plexiglas.

"Good grief, what the heck kind of training is this?" he asked himself out loud.

He looked around the room some more. Still, he was the only one present. Assuming he must be early, he found a seat in one of the back rows. As he sat down, it occurred to him that he might actually be in the wrong room. Maybe they got the signs mixed up and he was in an Early Childhood Educator Program or something.

He got up to leave just as a young man dressed in grey cargo pants and a white T-shirt walked to a podium on the stage in front of the jungle scene.

"Hi," he said. "I'm Chad… your facilitator for today's session." He paused, focusing on Ryan. "Hey Ryan, why don't you move up here?" he said motioning to the front of the room.

Ryan hesitated, "Noo, I'm good here. Thanks… but, by the way, where is everyone else?"

"This is everyone Ryan! It's the door you picked." He paused before continuing. "So, Ryan, I understand your boss feels this program will help you in your management role. Tell me a little about your job."

Ryan had no intention of discussing his job with this stranger, unless he wanted to know why he should be at the office instead of in front of some dumb forest scene.

"Not much to tell," he said. "It's your basic middle management position."

Chad seemed unconcerned with Ryan's response. "Well, maybe that's a chat for later," he said. "For now, let me take you through a bit about today's session. Here's the thing Ryan... Many mangers fall into the trap of trying to negotiate with everyone they meet but don't ever take time to negotiate with themselves. When I say 'negotiate with themselves,' I mean they don't take the time to do the type of reflection in which they consciously decide what their thoughts and actions are, or will be, rather than letting something or someone else decide that for them. They don't even realize they're not in control."

While Chad continued to talk about the session Ryan's mind went back to all the work he had waiting for him at his office. His budget was due, he had to do an orientation with a new employee, he started to dwell on Lance's cutting remarks at his performance review, and he began making a To-Do list in his head.

Suddenly, his thoughts were interrupted by a high-pitched squealing sound. He was shocked to see a monkey jumping from branch to branch on the trees behind the Plexiglas, but his attention was quickly diverted by Chad's voice while his eyes remained glued to the monkey jumping from branch to branch.

"Well Ryan, judging from our friend JoJo the chimp, we have a lot of work to do." Then JoJo left the stage. Ryan was still in a bit of shock over what had just occurred and responded with a rapid succession of questions.

"Excuse me, what was that all about? Was that a real monkey up there? Aren't there some health and safety regulations you're breaking here? And what was the point of all that anyway?"

Chad's response was calm and succinct. "Yes, that was, in fact, a real chimp. We're not in contravention of any health and safety regulations because JoJo is encased in Plexiglas. And by the end of today's session, you will be able to tell me yourself what the value was of having him join us today."

Lowering his voice to draw Ryan into the conversation, Chad then went on to outline some specific concerns Lance had about Ryan's management style.

"Ryan, I was told that your project team is getting frustrated. They say you spend a lot of time checking and responding to emails while in team meetings. They see you making lists while they're talking, and they don't feel you are really hearing their concerns or are even aware of their expertise. When someone asks you a question, you often ask them to repeat it, which tells them you weren't listening."

Ryan couldn't believe what he was hearing. This stranger, who knew nothing about him or his endless work load, was telling him he was a bad manager. His mind was flooded with thoughts about how many times he had diverted a crisis by multitasking during staff meetings, like the budget error he had caught, the impossible December deadline he had met, and dealing with the client who demanded immediate attention and was almost lost to a competitor. All those disasters were avoided because he multitasked during staff meetings.

The squealing sound of JoJo again interrupted his thoughts, drawing his attention to the stage. He looked up to see the chimp once again jumping from branch to branch of a huge tree. Ryan sat in silence, his eyes glued to the chimp until his attention was once again diverted by Chad's loud question.

"All that valuable information and you weren't listening to a word I was saying, were you Ryan?"

Ryan reverted to his defensive fall-back mode for dealing with what he considered to be blatant criticism.

"Seriously, a monkey jumping around squealing hardly counts as a learning experience," he said. "I've been here over an hour and haven't learned a thing."

"Haven't you?" Chad asked. "Let me ask you something Ryan. When I was introducing the session earlier, were you listening to what I was saying?"

Ryan hesitated. "Well, yes, I was sitting here wasn't I? I had no choice. I was your captive audience."

"Sorry Ryan, but I disagree. What else were you doing while you were listening? What were you thinking about?"

Ryan felt trapped. "Well, I guess I was thinking about my budget, and my new employee, and maybe something Lance, my manager, said a while ago."

"That's a lot of thinking. Tell me Ryan, do you remember what interrupted your thoughts."

"How can I forget, your friend JoJo of course."

"And a few minutes ago, what were you thinking about while I was talking about concerns expressed by your project team."

"I was listening, but I was also thinking about what my team was criticizing me for, multitasking, when that's exactly what keeps our department out of trouble. I can think about more than one thing at a time you know."

"Well, actually, according to neuroscience, you can't. When you think you're multitasking, what you are really doing is just shifting your focus from one task to another with great speed. To me that means you're not paying full attention to anything, which, in many cases, means more chance of missing something or doing a lesser quality job. And thinking about two things at the same time? Well, that simply isn't possible... Try it!"

"You mean right now?"

"Yes, please, go ahead and try to think of two things at the same time, not separately in lighting speed of each other, but at exactly the same time."

Ryan tried to think about buying gardening supplies later, and about dropping his mother's prescription off. "I guess you're right, I can't do it."

"Okay, and the next time you are on your phone, try to write an e-mail while you're also talking. See if you're really able to do two things at once. I mean exactly at the same time, not shifting your attention from one thing to the other."

Chad walked away from the podium and to the back of the room where Ryan was seated. He sat in a chair in the row in front of Ryan and turned to face him.

"Okay Ryan, I think you have a lot to share that you want me to know about. Go ahead... I'm listening."

Ryan was pleased he would finally have an opportunity to defend himself.

"I have to multitask! My work budget is due, I don't know if we will be able to hire any part-time staff, and Lance seems to think I am not doing a good job leading my team. On top of all of that, I have to deal with a new employee who's becoming a problem."

Once again, Ryan was startled by the sound of JoJo jumping from branch to branch.

"What the heck was that all about? Again!"

Chad scratched his chin. "Oh, sorry, I was thinking about having to pick up a birthday present for my wife after work, but please, go ahead, I'm listening."

Ryan looked at Chad and smiled a knowing smile. "Alright, I get it now. Every time we are thinking and not listening, the chimp comes out."

"Exactly! Bravo! You got it. Whenever you experience Monkey Mind JoJo comes out."

"Monkey what?"

As Chad walked back to the stage Ryan asked, "Seriously Chad, what is the point of all of this monkey business?"

"Let me tell you about Monkey Mind Ryan. Monkey Mind is when your mind jumps from thought to thought, just like JoJo jumps from branch to branch, not able to stay on any one branch very long. That's what the Buddhists call Monkey Mind, and it can sabotage our goals and our relationships, and reduce our potential for success.

"Part of this program will be to give you tools to deal with Monkey Mind, but also to help you identify other unconscious habits that sabotage your success. You see, our mind is like a monkey and will jump from thought to thought, like JoJo jumping from branch to branch without ever settling on any one branch. Most of us spend our lives living with thoughts of the past, which doesn't exist, or of the future, which also doesn't exist, instead of living in the present, paying attention to the now… the present moment. It's sad isn't it," he added. "We complain about how much time we don't have and yet we waste the time we do have living in a nonexistent future, or reliving the past. We might as well be in bed dreaming. It amounts to the same thing.

Tell me Ryan, does the past exist right now? Does what you did yesterday really exist now?"

"Well of course not," Ryan replied.

"So when I was talking on stage, every time JoJo interrupted was a time you were having random thoughts about Lance and what he said in the past, or about your budget and what was going to happen in the future, or about your new employee. But you weren't paying attention to what was happening in the present right here and now. We all do it! We all have random thoughts that don't serve us.

"In fact, that's what minds do, think random thoughts, unless we train the mind muscle. The majority of us let our minds wander on autopilot, keeping us living in the past or the future instead of in the present!"

Ryan recalled what Lance had told him about his team feeling he didn't listen to them, and his always being distracted by something else, like his lists and his cell phone. He wondered if maybe he really did have Monkey Mind.

"Well, if I do have Monkey Mind," he said, "and I'm not saying I do, but if did, what could I do about it?

"You saw how it was," Chad replied. "You were thinking about things that you had to deal with. Did you do that on purpose? Were you ignoring me on purpose?"

Chad lowered his voice. "The point is we don't do it intentionally. At those times, our minds are in control of our thoughts and we are not!"

Ryan started to feel a tinge of embarrassment. What Chad was saying made sense. He spent a lot of time thinking about things that had happened or about what might have gone wrong. Sometimes he spent a lot of time thinking about what had gone right and congratulating himself, but none of those thoughts were about anything in the present moment so, yes, he might as well have been dreaming. He often wasted the present by living in the past or the future.

"Maybe you're right Chad," he said. "Maybe I do live on autopilot and my mind controls me instead of me controlling my mind. I do spend a lot of time thinking about what will happen tomorrow or next week or next month or, sometimes, even next year. And you're right. Tomorrow doesn't exist, only what I do now counts."

Chad clapped his hands together. "BRAVO! Exactly!" he said as he looked at his watch. "So now Ryan, I'll let you go early today. You don't have to make up those 15 minutes, on one condition"

"What's that?"

"That you do the homework I give you… Do we have a deal?"

"Absolutely," Ryan said with a smile at the thought of being able to avoid the rush-hour traffic.

"Great! So here's your homework. When you leave here today, I want you to pay attention to your thoughts from the time you leave the Discovery Centre… on the way to your car, in the car, walking from your garage to the house, while you are having supper with your family, while you are talking to your wife, even while you are doing your groceries. Pay attention to what you are thinking about, and every time you find yourself thinking, ask yourself if it's past, present or future.

"If you answer past or future then you have to say 'Monkey Mind' to yourself, or out loud. Remember, you have to prevent thoughts of the past or future from invading your present, which is your real life. It is critical that you bring your thoughts back to the present, and whatever you are doing at the time." He paused a moment, then went on.

"Every time you bring your mind back to the present, you will be training it to live in the present and to stay on the present 'branch.' If your present is grocery shopping, then think about what you are doing. Look at the packaging whatever it is and be aware of the people around you, the sounds and the sights. If you are driving and catch yourself thinking about something other than driving, do the same thing. Consider whether your thoughts are in the past, the future, or the present."

"Well, what you say does make some sense," Ryan confessed. "The other day a student hit my car on his way to write an exam and I bet he wasn't thinking about the road or the traffic."

"Exactly... like missing where you were supposed to turn while driving somewhere?"

"Ya, in fact, just yesterday I was going to pick up my laundry on the way from work but instead I drove right past the turnoff and ended up heading straight home. An honest mistake for sure. After all, home is where I go every day after work, but I was thinking about my mother and if she'll be able to manage on her own for much longer.

"Hummm, I guess I was thinking about the non-existent future... Monkey Mind."

"Exactly," Chad agreed. "When your mind is scattered in the past and the future it's like a constant low-grade stress that you're not even conscious of, like the way some people constantly have the TV on, even though no one's watching it. It's just background noise that doesn't allow for a quiet, peaceful environment... constant low-grade noise pollution."

"But Chad," Ryan broke in, "Sometimes you have to plan the future... like I need to do my taxes and figure out if I can buy a second car. I need to do that in the present, and I need to think about the options my mother will have if she can't live alone anymore."

"Good point Ryan. Yes, sometimes we have to plan for the future in the present, and that's perfectly fine, but instead of it being a constant low-grade background thought that pops up randomly, you need to decide where and when you will do that planning and then sit down and do it at the time chosen by you. Monkey Mind should not be deciding for you. Remember, you should control your mind; your mind should not control you."

"Okay, I get it," Ryan said. "So tell me more about this homework you want me to do. I don't want to get caught in rush-hour traffic."

"Well, Part 2 of your homework assignment is this. When you are having dinner with your family tonight, I want you to stay in the present moment. Tell me Ryan, what are you usually thinking about while you're eating?"

"What I'm going to do after supper, of course… or something that happened at work that made me mad or glad. Yes, I know! I guess I am living in the nonexistent past and missing my life. Monkey Mind!"

"Wow!" Chad said with delight. "I couldn't have said it better myself. Yup, exactly that! You are missing your life. You are missing precious time with your family that you can never get back.

"So tonight I want you to look at the food before you eat and think about all the work gone into preparing it, all the people it took to get that meal to your table, especially the loving hands that cooked it. Then I want you to taste it… really taste it… first with your eyes, then take in the smell, the texture on your tongue and, and finally, the taste. It's not just about tasting your food; it's also about what happens when you force yourself to stay present and experience it in the present moment.

"Then, of course, make sure you are present with your family. Listen, give them your presence, the most important gift you can give, and enjoy time with them over the meal."

"Okay, I totally see your point," Ryan said. "When you are living in the present you are actually living your life, not reliving a nonexistent past or anticipating your next activity in the nonexistent future.

"When you think about it, the future doesn't exist because when it gets here, it's the present. But I don't have a button I can just click, like turning the TV off, that will stop my mind from thinking about the past or the future."

"Oh, but there are buttons you can click," Chad said. "But that's for tomorrow's session. For now, when you find yourself with Monkey Mind I want you to take three deep breaths and feel the air as you inhale it. Then redirect your attention to the present moment, whatever you are doing."

"Hmmm," Ryan pondered. "You totally lost me there."

"Okay, you can use your breath as an anchor to redirect your attention to the present. So when you find yourself in Monkey Mind status, take three deep breaths, which should be sufficient to redirect your attention to whatever you are doing. I call it the one, two, three redirect."

If you have to redirect five times in a minute, bravo! That's okay. Go for it! What's important is recognizing you are not living in the present."

"What do you mean 'Bravo'? It's obviously not working if I have to redirect myself five times in one minute."

"But it is working Ryan. Each time you have to redirect yourself to the present moment you are strengthening your mind muscle. It's like any other muscle in your body. Have you ever gone to the gym?"

"I did do some work on my biceps last summer."

"Okay then. Was it hard? Did your muscles get sore?"

"Well, it was really hard in the beginning. My muscles were really sore, but then after a while it got easier and easier until one day I had built my biceps up to where I wanted them to be, and I just had to maintain it."

"Exactly… It works the same way with building your mind muscle. At first it might be really hard and you may get frustrated at how many times you have to redirect yourself to the present. But don't be angry about it; be glad because every time you redirect yourself to the present it's like lifting weights to build up that mind muscle."

"Okay, got it," Ryan said as he got up and started heading toward the door.

"Yes, it's time to hit the road. We don't want to get caught in rush-hour traffic. Don't forget to pick up your phone."

"Ya, about that," Ryan said turning back to Chad." Can you do anything about my phone… I'm serious? I just can't afford to not have access to my office."

"Ryan, have you heard about the research linking similarities between using cocaine and using technology?"

Ryan laughed. "You're kidding, right?"

"No, I'm serious," Chad said emphatically. "In fact, that's what caused me to start putting my cell phone away for at least a couple of hours a day, at lunch time and in the evening, until at least after supper."

Ryan listened with interest as Chad explained the research on people addicted to technology and began to worry about the amount of time he let little Tara spend on her tablet playing games, and she was only eight. In fact, he realized he kind of used the laptop as a babysitter whenever it was his turn to take care of Tara during her play time.

"Wow! That's serious stuff," he said as he turned to the door again. "I thought you were just kidding. I doubt I'm addicted, but hey, I'll keep an eye on it."

"One more thing Ryan," Chad said, stopping him once again. "I have a little something for you to take home."

He reached into his pocket and pulled out a plastic card. "Here, this is for you. Put it where you will see it often, especially first thing in the morning."

"Thank you Chad," Ryan said as he looked at the large print on the card:

"Life is what happens to you while you're busy making other plans."

"Thanks," he repeated. "It's so true… I know just the place to put it."

"It's my pleasure Ryan. See you tomorrow."

Ryan retrieved his phone from the white box and put the electronic bracelet back. As he exited the doors of the Discovery Centre he caught himself going through the mental traffic of thoughts about what he needed to do that evening. Immediately, he caught himself in the future. *'Monkey Mind!'* he said under his breath and quickly diverted his attention to the walk to his car.

On the way he saw some lilac bushes off to the side of the building and noticed the breezy spring air was laced with their scent. As he opened the car door, with a smile he said to himself, *'Building my mind muscle.'*

He drove out of the parking lot and soon after stopped the car so a gaggle of geese could safely cross the street. Rather than his usual impatience at having to wait, he focused on watching three baby geese waddling along at the end of the line. With the last of them safely across, he pulled out onto the street.

A few minutes later he switched on the radio and then, remembering what Chad had said about TVs being background noise pollution, he turned it off again. With some effort, he managed to focus on driving and the sights and sounds as he made his way to the pharmacy to pick up his mother's prescription. He entered the pharmacy parking lot with thoughts of her declining ability to live on her own and began reliving the recent scare he had had when she fell and broke her hip.

Ryan was the only one of her offspring who lived close to his mother. The others were several hours away, so he was the one she depended on for everything. He was used to dropping off groceries or medication, or taking her to medical appointments.

His mother, now 79, often looked at him with longing in her eyes and would ask, "Can't you stay for a bite to eat?" But he always had the same reply. "Sorry mum, it's been a long day, and it's not done yet."

Predictably she always replied, "That's okay, I know how busy you are dear."

Ryan always felt a little guilty as he shut the door behind him, but he just wanted to get home, put on some comfortable sweats and get to work on his most immediate project. Being able to take off his suit and put on sweats before moving on to the next deadline was his idea of relaxing.

As he waited for the pharmacist to fill the prescription he found himself getting more concerned about what would have happened if he had not gone by his mother's to drop off groceries on the day she fell. He felt his stomach tighten. And once again, he caught himself living in the past. *'Monkey Mind!'* Still, he continued to relive the incident.

Recognizing what a strong hold his thoughts had on him, he found himself using Chad's suggestion and under his breath said, "One, two, three, redirect." As he took three deep breaths, feeling the air flow through his nostrils and into his lungs. It worked! He was able to redirect his thoughts to where he actually was… at the pharmacy. He reminded himself that he was getting a prescription filled for his healthy mother.

"Here you go," the pharmacist said, passing him the medication.

"Thank you," he replied with a smile.

As he got into the car, Ryan felt a sense of relief that he could choose not to continue reliving that awful evening when he arrived at his mother's house and found her on the kitchen floor unable to move. Besides, he thought, she now had the medic alert around her neck. Should that ever happen again all she has to do is press the button and an ambulance will come and they will call him.

It was a more restful ride home than usual and, as he stepped into the foyer of his house, Tara ran up to greet him. He consciously paused for a moment to enjoy her small arms reaching to give him a hug.

That evening he was determined to complete his homework assignment while having dinner. In fact, he was somewhat curious as to whether it might even have an impact on his entire evening. He looked down at his plate and spent a moment appreciating the feast before his eyes—orange baby carrots, baked chicken, mashed potatoes, gravy and corn.

Then, as Chad had suggested, he inhaled the aroma and his mouth watered at the mere sight and smell. As he brought the food to his lips he remembered to spend time enjoying the texture and the taste.

"Wow! I do say this meal is scrumptious! Wouldn't you agree Tara?"

"Oh yes Dad, Mummy's the best cook in the whole world."

Ryan smiled and looked over at Leela, who was surprised by his complimentary and attentive behaviour.. It occurred to him with some surprise that he never thanked her for the daily meals she made with such care.

"Yes Tara, I would have to agree, your mum is the best in the East, and in the West." He winked at Leela, whose eyes twinkled a thank-you in return.

Ryan continued to pay attention to the taste and texture of the meal while conversing in between mouthfuls with Leela and Tara. Once he got the hang of really paying attention to the rituals of dinnertime, and actually tasting and appreciating the food before him, he found that it actually tasted more delicious than usual. Only twice did thoughts of the future arise during the meal, and he was able to use "One, two, three, redirect, breathing" to return to the present moment.

"Hey Tara, I noticed you're gobbling your food up really fast, how about we play a game of tell me what it looks like, feels like, tastes like, and smells like."

Tara enjoyed playing the new tasting game with her dad and Leela joined in on the fun.

"Wow!" Tara said at one point. "How come the food tastes different... better than usual?"

Realizing it was a good teachable moment, he replied. "I also think it tastes better... Maybe it's because we are paying more attention to eating and tasting and appreciating the delicious meal your mum prepared, instead of just gobbling it up fast so you can go out to play and I can get back to my laptop."

As the meal came to an end, Tara asked, "Dad, are you coming to my recital on Friday?"

"Oh, I totally forgot about that," he said.

"But Dad, how could you forget such an important thing again? Didn't you put it in your calendar with all your other important things?"

She looked as if she was about to cry. She had a small role in a play at the recital and had been practicing every day after school for the past week.

"I'm sorry my angel," he said. "I will do my best... In fact, let me check my calendar right now." He pulled out his cell phone but then quickly put it back in his pocket as he pronounced: "No electronics at the table! It's a new rule. I will try to fit it into my schedule after dinner."

"That's great," Tara said with delight. "Thanks Dad."

After dinner Ryan stayed behind to help Leela clear up the dishes, something she usually did on her own.

"So, I didn't get a chance to tell you," Leela said as she began scrubbing dishes in the sink, "but Jerry has been diagnosed with Alzheimer's. It's so sad. Susan was going to retire this year, then they would both be retired, and they had planned to travel across Europe. So sad... all those years of planning. You know she put $100 every paycheque into bonds for their travels."

As Leela was talking Ryan's mind started to drift to the audit report he had to read. He heard her voice in the background of his thoughts and caught himself.

'Monkey Mind is back,' he thought to himself. *'One, two, three, redirect.'*

And with that he was back in the present with Leela, drying dishes and listening to her with present moment awareness. It was a good feeling.

Chapter 2

Switching From Autopilot to Manual

Your thoughts can fuel your success ...or feed your failure

Ryan woke up to sunshine streaming through the bedroom window. As he found his way to the bathroom he was already wondering if he should talk to Lance about the audit report. There were a few areas of concern that would not reflect well on the department and should be attended to, but as he was brushing his teeth Ryan noticed the card taped to the mirror where he had put it the night before.

> *"Life is what happens to you while you're busy making other plans."*

"Monkey Mind!" he said out loud, immediately realizing he had just been living in the nonexistent future. Even the boring process of brushing his teeth was preferable to living in a nonexistent future. Besides, he knew at a gut level that decisions made while multitasking were not likely going to be as good as decisions made with focused attention. Now, apparently, research backed that up.

'Monkey Mind is back!' He took three deep breaths and redirected his attention to brushing his teeth with precision. He noticed his gums were receding, something he hadn't noticed before, and he had missed his annual dental check-up this year.

It was an odd experience for him, this present-moment awareness, even with brushing his teeth—the spearmint taste and smell of the toothpaste, the feel of the bristles against his teeth. All these things he had never paid attention to were suddenly noticeable to his senses.

He moved on to shaving, which Ryan was very precise about, so it was a long, tedious task that made him look forward to the weekend when he didn't shave.

Ryan could see Leela's robe in the bathroom mirror hanging on the back of the bathroom door. He had to decide on an anniversary present for her. He wanted to get something that would be meaningful. She always got him such sentimental gifts. She always put so much thought into presents. His favourite was a first edition of Kipling's *Jungle Book*.

Then there was the scrapbook with pictures of him and Tara taken from the day she was born to his recent birthday, and a framed shot for his office of her baby hand prints and her 10-year-old handprints side by side.

On the other hand, his gifts were always practical. He usually came up with them during the drive home from work. On her last birthday, he got her a new curling iron because her old one had broken.

"Ouch!" Bright red blood trickled down his neck and he immediately remembered what Chad had told him about focusing on whatever he was doing at the moment and living in the present.

"Monkey Mind again!" he said as he reached for a cotton ball.

Later, as he opened the door to his car to head off to work, Ryan was determined to focus on driving. He thought about his recent car accident. The person in the other car was a student worried about getting to class on time. How ironic! His rush probably caused him to not make it to the exam at all. Had he been focused on driving, the accident likely would not have occurred. It didn't matter how much thinking the kid did about it, or worrying about it, he would get there when he got there. Instead, he missed his exam altogether, and it cost him money for car repairs.

'Monkey Mind!' As the words surfaced in his mind, Ryan was surprised at how often he was actually

living in a nonexistent past or future, how easily his mind wandered, how often he was not living his actual present experiences.

"One two three, redirect," he said.

As he pulled into his parking spot at the office he thought about how his team would respond to his analysis of the audit report, if they would agree with him. Immediately, he started to feel anxious but his anxiety led him, once again, to recognize he wasn't living in the present moment. He anchored his thoughts with his breath and said, "One two three, redirect!"

As he entered his office, Ryan was greeted by Ron, his administrative assistant.

"Hi, how is your morning so far?" he asked Ryan.

"Good," he replied, and realized he actually meant it. "Although I was surprised to see that we're spending money on an electronic billboard," he added. "When did they put that up?"

"Oh… about six months ago," Ron said.

Ryan was surprised, and a bit embarrassed. He drove into that same parking lot every day but this was the first time he had noticed the billboard.

"I have copies of the report for you to distribute to the team, and here is the agenda for our meeting," Ron said.

"Thanks Ron."

As he walked out the door Ryan grabbed the papers where Ron had put them and minutes later he was sitting at the boardroom table surrounded by his team.

As he waited for the stragglers to arrive, he began to think about how the last meeting went and felt his stomach tighten. It was that last team meeting that Lance was referring to when he said his team had complained about him. The tightening in Ryan's stomach cued him to check his present moment awareness and, as he suspected, Monkey Mind was at play.

'One, two three, redirect!' Ryan yanked himself back into the present and almost immediately had an out-of-the-box idea that he would put into effect right away.

"Hello everyone… beautiful morning, isn't it?" he asked rhetorically, then paused briefly. "Let's take a minute today and clear our minds before we start, so we can better focus on today's agenda items."

Everyone looked at him with obvious confusion, and then at each other. Ryan's typical way of starting a meeting was by tapping his pen on the table and saying something like, "Okay, we have a full agenda so let's get to it!" At which point the room would go silent.

Seeing the confused looks on their faces, Ryan lowered his voice and offered an explanation.

"I know we all are coming from other places and other meetings and going to other meetings after this one. It can be hard to transition from one to the other with so many thoughts on our minds so let's just take a couple of minutes and clear our minds. Ryan looked down at his watch, so for the next five minutes, think about what you want to get out of this meeting and what you want to leave this meeting with."

Ryan didn't notice that Lance was standing outside the open boardroom door, listening to his instructions to his team. Lance smiled an all-knowing smile of satisfaction. He always thought Ryan really had it in him to be a great manager, but others in the senior management team had their doubts.

After five minutes, Ryan opened the audit report and in a friendly tone said, "Okay, let's begin."

He led his team through the agenda more efficiently than usual, and his team provided him with more input than usual. When he saw the red light flashing on his phone indicating that he had an email waiting, he quickly turned it face down and redirected his attention to a team member, Jordon, who was talking.

Ryan usually didn't pay much attention to what Jordon had to say. He considered the long-winded build-up in which he repeated what everyone else had already said to be annoying and a waste of time.

Today was no different. As Jordon continued to speak, Ryan found himself wondering what the afternoon would be like at Discovery Centre. He wondered if he would get to pick another door. Maybe this time he would pick Who Hijacked My Emotions, or Ryan in Wonderland.

Someone in the meeting had forgotten to turn off their phone and it's ringing jarred Ryan back to the present moment. *'Monkey Mind,'* he thought to himself. *'One, two, three, redirect.'*

He forced himself to refocus on what Jordon was saying only to find he was still not finished his review of everyone's comments. As he did his best to listen intently he caught an error in something Jordon said.

"Excuse me," he interrupted. "I think you misunderstood what Sharon said earlier. Sharon, is that what you meant?"

Sharon looked up in surprise at hearing her name. "What? Sorry, I must have missed that."

Ryan recognized that Monkey Mind was at play in Sharon's mind, and maybe others' as well.

"Didn't you say you would be able to complete Phase 2 by October?" he asked her.

"Umm... Yes, yes I did," she said.

"Jordon thought you said March."

"No, definitely October."

"Sorry, my mistake," Jordon said, looking a little embarrassed. "I must have missed that... Well, that changes things then."

Ryan was thankful he had quickly regained focus on what Jordon was saying and realized there was some value to all of his repetition after all... if people are actually listening to it... and it seemed Sharon had not been.

With that realization, he thought how valuable it would be for his whole team to take a workshop on Monkey Mind. In fact, maybe he would recommend they attend the next scheduled program.

"Well, that was the last item on our agenda," he announced when everyone had had an opportunity to speak. "Thank you for your work on this project. See you all next month."

Before long it was time for him to leave for the Discovery Centre. As he crossed the parking lot, he looked up at the electronic billboard and shook his head in disbelief that he could have missed that huge monstrosity for six months. *'Monkey Mind, that's how,'* he thought to himself.

Traffic on the way to the Discovery Centre was slower than usual for lunch hour and Ryan caught himself in his habitual pattern of becoming frustrated. He found himself talking to drivers who were oblivious to his existence. When he looked at his watch and realized he had more than enough time to get there, he chuckled to himself in a moment of Eureka. He was living on autopilot. All his life he secretly took pride on being disciplined and effective, but here he was, slammed with the realization that he was living on autopilot... like Pavlov's dogs.

With that, he began to inwardly criticize himself. *'I'm supposed to be the disciplined, self-sufficient one. Me living on autopilot? I might as well be a mindless pattern of behaviours and emotions. Me? Controlled by the past and nonexistent future? How could that be, autopilot is what hormone-laden teenagers are all about, not disciplined adults!'*

He was still in a state of disappointment with himself as he pulled into the parking lot of the Discovery Centre. As he entered the building he found himself again walking at a rushed pace as if he were late, even though he had a good 15 minutes to spare. With the unwarranted feeling of urgency, he sensed he might be in Monkey Mind yet again. *'One, two, three, redirect.'* He summoned himself back to the present.

As he entered the circular white room and shut the door behind him, he walked over to the white leather chair and sank into it with a sigh. Soon after, the familiar voice came over the intercom.

"Welcome Ryan. We will be with you in 15 minutes. Please place your phone in the white box and spend some time relaxing, clearing and preparing your mind for this afternoon's session."

Still a bit resentful of having to give up his phone for the afternoon, Ryan noticed the red light blinking on it. As he started to enter his password he remembered the story of Pavlov's dog, and JoJo jumping about in the Plexiglas enclosure. He stood up quickly and placed the phone in the white box and saw that the wrist band was no longer there. He didn't think much of it. The low-grade anxiety he often felt was replaced by a sense of victory as he locked the box.

'I'm no Pavlovian dog,' he thought to himself as he sank into the comfy leather chair once again.

"Please spend the next 15 munities relaxing and clearing your mind to prepare for this afternoon's session," said the voice on the intercom.

Ryan complied and sat quietly looking around the room. The bare white walls offered a bit of comfort to his jumble of thoughts but every time he closed his eyes in an attempt to relax, a thought came to him and he had to use one, two, three, redirect over and over. He started getting frustrated with this random coming and going of thoughts until he remembered Chad saying that every time he had to redirect he was actually strengthening his mind muscle.

Finally, the door to the round room opened slowly and quietly as Lance entered.

"Hi, Mila said I could come in. She said your 15 minutes of down time is complete."

Ryan laughed. "Down time hey? Well, I have to say I do feel a bit more relaxed than when I first arrived." However, on seeing Lance, he also remembered the lingering sense of anger with him ever since his performance review.

"So how was your morning? Did you keep the monkey off your back?" Lance asked with a chuckle.

Ryan felt embarrassed recalling the number of times he heard himself thinking *'Monkey Mind'* throughout the morning. He shared those instances with Lance, along with the times when he had found himself on autopilot.

"To be honest," he said. "I'm so pissed off with myself. I can't believe how often I'm in the Monkey Mind world. I really thought I was more disciplined than that."

Lance put a hand on Ryan's shoulder. "Don't be upset with yourself Ryan. It's natural for your mind to jump from thought to thought. That's what minds do.

Your job is to train your mind muscle to know you're in control. Hey remember that time you decided to quit smoking? How long did it take you to finally quit?"

"About 10 months," Ryan replied. "Do you remember when you first started? How hard it was, how frustrated you would get?"

"It was one of the hardest thing I ever did, especially when I drank beer."

"So did you get angry at yourself because it was tough?"

"No, of course not… In fact, I was pretty pleased when I was able to resist the urge, and so was Leela. The more I did the easier it would get!

"Exactly," Lance agreed. "And look at you now, a non-smoker. Well I have to get back to my own session now," he said as turned to leave, then asked, "Have you chosen your door for today?"

Ryan was surprised to find himself a bit excited at picking a door. "Ya, I'm going for, Ryan in Wonderland."

Chapter 3

Ryan in Wonderland

"The mind is a wonderful servant, but a terrible master."
Robin Sharma

Ryan opened the door of his choice and entered what appeared to be a movie theatre with a huge screen at the front and the strong smell of hot popcorn everywhere.

"Welcome, care for some popcorn?"

"Hi Chad," Ryan said, relieved to see a familiar face. Again, he was the only one in the theatre.

Chad handed him a bag of fresh popcorn.

"Thanks, am I in the right room? This is the Negotiation With Yourself Program, right?"

"Sure is! Have a seat Ryan, and don't sit in the very back row again, okay?"

Ryan chuckled and changed his direction toward the middle of the theatre. Chad followed and sat beside him. After getting comfortable, Ryan adjusted his eyes to the dim lighting. Scanning the far right side of the theatre, he noticed what looked like four life-size photos of a person mounted on the wall. He squinted, remembering he had to make an appointment to see the optometrist.

His attention was quickly diverted to the screen at the front of the room when one of his favourite songs, Harry Chapin's *Cats in the Cradle* started playing while the title, *Ryan in Wonderland* flashed on the screen.

Chad leaned in and whispered to Ryan, "Here it comes… it's movie time!"

Ryan wondered why Chad bothered to whisper since they were the only ones in the theatre.

A video of Ryan and Leela bringing Tara home from the hospital was on the screen.

"Hey, that's Tara, my daughter. Wow, I remember that day like it was yesterday." He felt the same joy bubbling up inside of him as he did the day she was born.

Seeing the pride on Ryan's face, Chad said, "Oh, she's obviously your bundle of joy. I can see that… Look at you smiling from ear to ear proud papa."

Ryan was so moved watching the video, even though it was 8 years ago, he relived every moment of happiness like it was yesterday. The love he felt for Tara welled up inside of him.

The song ended and a new one began. It was one of his dad's favourites. He would play it while they worked together in the garage: Garth Brooks, *The Dance*.

Then the presentation shifted to another video that Ryan had taken himself while his dad was in the hospital. He watched as images of his father hugging his daughter came on, along with images of her waving as they celebrated what would be his dad's last Father's Day.

He recalled the day the doctors told him his father's cancer was terminal. The months and the sorrow that followed came flooding back to him. He went from a state of joy recalling Tara's entry into his life to one of pain and sadness with thoughts of the slow, painful disease that took his father's life. He remembered the daily visits, watching his dad deteriorate day by day, yet struggling to be brave for his mum, Tara and Leela.

Ryan felt his eyes welling up with tears. As he yanked his mind out of what seemed like a dream, on the brink of tears and his face flushed, he turned to Chad in anger.

"What the hell is this, some kind of sick joke?"

"Ryan… I understand this must be upsetting to watch, but it's necessary for this session."

"No kidding it's upsetting," Ryan retorted. "Where did you get these videos anyway?"

"It really doesn't matter where the videos came from. What matters is that they will help you to uncover a secret that will revolutionize your thinking."

The theatre lights turned up a bit as the music tapered off. Ryan pulled himself together and sat up straight.

"Okay, as difficult as it may be Ryan, I need you to stop, listen, and think."

"What? Like in kindergarten? Stop, listen, and think about what?"

"Do you ever think about what you are thinking about?" Chad asked.

"Look, I'm not in the mood for trick questions Chad. Haven't you screwed with me enough for one day? I can't believe I'm wasting time here watching home movies."

"Listen Ryan, I understand you are upset, but there is a bigger picture here, one that will change your life. Tell you what. Give me an open mind for the next hour. Put aside your anger just for one hour and answer my questions honestly and with an open mind. If you do this, you can choose to end the program today and I will give you the certificate of completion."

"You're serious? One hour, and I'm out of here?"

Ryan thought about all the extra work he could get done if he only spent an hour with Chad. He would have the rest of the day free without a single meeting. He could catch up on so much work.

"Yup, just one more hour of your time, an open mind, and honest responses… but you can't just go through the motions. You have to be committed to being open to the possibility that something good can come out of what you just experienced."

Ryan hesitated for a minute, a little calmer now.

"Okay," he said, "one hour. You got it. My mind is as open as it'll ever be… and I'll answer your questions."

"Honestly?"

Ryan hesitated before offering a reluctant, "Yes, honestly."

"Great! Let's go back to the question I asked you."

"Oh yes, the trick question," Ryan said.

"No, Ryan, a life question. In fact, I will use the Socratic method with you for the next hour."

"The what?"

"The Socratic method," Chad replied. "It was used by Socrates as a teaching tool in which the teacher asks continuous probing questions intended to explore the student's beliefs. In this case, we want to explore how you view your thoughts. So let's get back to that first question. Do you ever think about what you are thinking about?"

"Sure," Ryan said, "I think about lots of things, like a few minutes ago when you decided to torment me with pictures of my dying father, I was thinking about how no one should have to end their life that way, and how he would never see Tara grow up, never attend her graduations, or her wedding."

"Yes, I am sorry we had to play that video, but we also showed the day Tara made her entrance into the world."

Chad stood up and started walking to the far side of the theatre where the life-size photos were that Ryan had noticed earlier. As they approached the photos together, still a little agitated, Ryan asked, "What the heck is this all about Chad?"

"Don't get distracted by the photos," Chad looked concerned.. "I need you to focus on the questions I am going to ask you. Remember our deal."

"Don't get distracted? Chad, there are four life-size photos of me on the wall… Hey, that picture was taken at our 10-year service-recognition lunch, wasn't it?

I was wearing that new white linen shirt Leela gave me for our twelfth anniversary."

"Let's just get past the photos, shall we," Chad said. "They're just props to help make my point. Now tell me how you felt when you walked into the theatre today?"

Ryan hesitated, but remembering their deal, he made his best effort to keep an open mind about this so-called Socratic teaching method.

"Well, I guess I was curious about whether I would learn anything useful, like yesterday's session. I was even a little excited to see what was behind the door I had chosen."

Chad walked over to the first photo and wrote on it, *"Curious, Excited (9 a.m.)."*

Now tell me how you felt when you saw the video of Tara?"

"I felt happy, full of love, you might even say full of joy and gratitude."

"Okay, okay, that's good," Chad responded as he walked over to the second photo and wrote, *"Happy, Love, Joy, Gratitude (9:15)."*

"Now, I know it may be difficult, but tell me how you felt when you saw the videos of your dad."

Ryan's furrowing brow causing his eyes to squint as he replied. "How the hell do you think I felt… like crap… like someone kicked me in the stomach when I wasn't looking! Like my stomach was in knots, like I was reliving the worst time of my life… sad, depressed, and horrified! Should I go on!"

"I want you to be honest and have an open mind Ryan."

Ryan lowered his voice to a whisper, as if he was speaking in secrecy.

"To be honest, I started to tear up and then I felt embarrassed, and I thought about how sadistic you were subjecting me to that, then I got angry."

"Okay, that's good honest reflection. Thank you."

Chad picked up a marker and walked over to the next life-size photo of Ryan and wrote on it, "*Sad, Depressed, Horrified, Stomach in Knots, Angry (9:30)."*

"And how are you feeling now?"

"No offence, but if I have to be honest, I'm a bit pissed off and confused. I mean, I don't see the point of all these questions. I've been here for over an hour now and I don't feel we've accomplished anything."

Chad walked over to the forth image and wrote the words, "*Annoyed, Confused (9:45)."*

"Okay Ryan, I want you to look at these four images of yourself and tell me what you see?"

"Well, a good looking guy?"

Chad laughed in appreciation of Ryan's effort to lighten the mood.

"Seriously, what do you notice when you look at them."

Ryan's brow furrowed again as he examined the words on each photo.

"What do I see... I see me having a lot of different emotions."

Chad, appearing to be deep in thought, replied after some hesitation. "Okay, my second question: "How long has it been since you walked into the theatre?"

Ryan pulled back the sleeve of his sweater so he could see his watch.

"Nice watch," Chad commented.

"Thanks. Actually, it's my favourite. I have a bit of a watch collection but I rarely wear them now because I always have my phone with me to check the time.

Well… except you people won't allow phones so I'm back to the old fashioned way."

Chad laughed at the thought of watches being old fashioned. "Isn't that interesting, how technology changes our behaviour sometimes without us even thinking about it. When was the last time you wore that watch before today… and when was the last time you bought a watch for your watch collection?"

"Geee," Ryan pondered. "Come to think of it, I haven't bought a new watch for at least a couple of years now, and even Leela stopped buying them for birthday and Christmas presents like she used to. Come to think of it, this is the first time since… let's see… since my birthday that I even wore a watch. Leela insisted that I leave my cell phone at home when we went out for dinner, but she took hers in case the babysitter needed to get hold of us."

"Well there's some food for thought… on your own time," Chad laughed before moving the conversation on. "So, as I was asking, about how long have you been here today?"

Ryan glanced at his watch again. "About an hour and a half, I guess."

"So let's think about that for a few minutes," Chad said as he walked over to the photo wall. "You said you experienced a bunch of emotional states. In an hour and a half you went from feeling excited when you walked into the room, to joyful and happy, to depressed and sad, to aggravated, to angry, to being on the brink of tears, and all that time you were in the same room with just one person at a leadership training program."

Chad paused and looked intently at the photos in silence, which was finally broken by the slow, quiet opening of the door.

"Ah, Lance," Chad said as he turned to the door. "Perfect timing! We're just getting to the good part. Come join us."

Ryan was peeved to have Lance join the session. His presence made him uncomfortable and somewhat anxious. He started thinking about the performance appraisal and how unfair Lance had been in his evaluation of the way he led his team. He remained certain that Lance didn't think he was ready for a senior management position.

Lance took a seat beside Ryan as he asked, "So Ryan, how's it going. Are you pleased with your choice of doors for today?"

Surprised at how genuinely happy Lance seemed to be to see him, Ryan replied. "So far it's been a very interesting afternoon. You were right about this not being your typical training set up."

"Yes, indeed," Lance agreed. "It's not every day you have four life-size photos of yourself staring back at you."

"I hate to break up the chat guys," Chad broke in, "but we have some work to do here."

"Oh, sorry," Lance responded. "Let me say my goodbyes then… just wanted to check in. See you tomorrow Ryan."

"Okay, back to work then," Chad said, shifting his attention back to the photos and pointing to the writing on each of the photos..

"So, as I was saying, you've experienced emotions ranging from joy to being on the brink of tears, and all that time you've been in the same room with the same person, at a leadership program."

Ryan folded his arms and looked intently at the photos again. "Hmmm, I guess you're right, that is odd. I never really pay attention to how I am feeling but… Wow! That's a lot of emotions to experience in just an hour and a half."

"Good, I like that open mind of yours. So now let's go back to the initial question I asked you. Do you ever think about what you are thinking about?"

"Back to the trick question… Let me think about that of a minute."

After a brief pause, he continued. "Do I, Ryan, ever think about… the thoughts I am thinking? Do I ever think about the thoughts I am thinking?

He pondered the question for a long time before going on and then blurted, "Yes! I would say the answer is yes.. Yes, I have thoughts and yes, I think them."

Chad shifted from in front of the photos and sat down beside Ryan. "This is critical Ryan, so let's think about it carefully," he said.

"You, Ryan, have thoughts, so then Ryan and Ryan's thoughts are two separate things… True or false?"

He looked intently at Ryan for his answer but Ryan was flustered, not sure what Chad was getting at. He felt he was being put on the spot to answer without having enough time to sufficiently consider the question or his response.

"Really," he finally said, "what is this Chad? I feel like I'm in school and being tested."

"Well, think about that a minute. Isn't life kind of like a huge school? Every morning your wake up and go out into the world, a world that has many lessons to teach… if we pay attention. The problem is that most people don't pay attention. They just keep living on autopilot making the same mistakes over and over.

"As Einstein said, *"The definition of insanity is doing the same thing over and over again, but expecting different results."*

"Hey, I think I'll use that at my next team meeting," Ryan said.

"Sure, and while you're at it, maybe explain this. If people took a moment to ask themselves, 'What is the lesson in this failure?' maybe they would do better. The school of life has many lessons to teach but when things go wrong most people look around to see who they can blame, and that overrides all the value in the learning opportunity... in the perceived error.

"For many people," he added, "their thoughts automatically go to the question, 'Who is to blame for this?' And that's an autopilot response."

He paused a moment while Ryan digested what he had said, then he went on. "But I'm sorry, I digress. So what's it going to be Ryan, true or false?"

"Hmmm, can you repeat the question again?"

"Ryan and Ryan's thoughts are two different things. True or false?"

"True," he said. "No, false... Yes, false is my answer."

"Are you sure about that Ryan? You are saying that your thoughts are you, that Ryan and Ryan's thoughts are the same thing. In other words, you are your thoughts. Is that what you are saying then?"

"Well, yes. That's what I'm saying."

"Okay then, let me ask you this. You are aware of your thoughts. True or false?"

"Yes, true!"

"Are your thoughts aware of you?"

"Seriously Chad, what kind of question is that? Rhetorical obviously."

"No, I want you to think about that.

You said you are your thoughts, that Ryan and Ryan's thoughts are the same thing, so you are your thoughts and your thoughts are you. Is that what you said?"

"Well, yes, I and my thoughts are one and the same thing."

"But if that's true, how come you are aware of your thoughts but your thoughts are not aware of you?"

"Hmmm... interesting," Ryan replied. "I never thought of it that way. It's like... I am aware of my hand but my hand is not aware of me. I am aware of my mouth but my mouth is not aware of me. I'm aware of my thoughts but my thoughts are not aware of me. Gee, this is a bit more complex than I thought it would be."

Chad remained silent as Ryan hesitated while he looked at the four life-size photos of himself and the words boldly written across each.

"Curious, Excitement... joyful, happy... sadness, depression, tears... anger..."

"Now that I am reviewing those photos," he began again, "I am thinking maybe I will change my answer. Look at all those feelings I experienced in an hour, and now I am thinking about how I managed to go through so many different emotions at a mere leadership training program of all places... and with no beer!"

Chad laughed as he asked, "So what's your final answer Ryan?"

"My final answer is false."

Suddenly a symphony of bells went off, as if he was in a game show and had just won the grand prize. At that moment, the theatre screen flashed the message:

YOU ARE NOT YOUR THOUGHTS!

THINK ABOUT WHAT YOU'RE THINKING ABOUT

Experts say we have 50,000-70,000 thoughts a day. That's 35-48 thoughts per minute crowding your mind!

Ryan looked in disbelief at the last statement.

"Wow! So that means if I'm talking to someone for five minutes, each of us will have 35-48 thoughts per minute. So in just five minutes, at a minimum, each of us will have at least 175 thoughts. No wonder people have Monkey Mind!"

"Okay Ryan, three more true or false questions. Get these right and we're done! You can choose to skip the rest of the program and still get your certificate of completion. Ready?"

"As ready as I'll ever be!"

"When Ryan came into the Discovery Centre today he was curious. True or false?"

"True."

"When Ryan saw the video of the day that he took his daughter home for the first time, he was joyful and happy. True or false?"

"True."

When Ryan saw the video of his father in the hospital, he was depressed, sad, and angry. True or false?

"True."

"Is that your final answer for all three?"

"Yes, those were easy… pretty obvious answers I would say. Those are my final answers."

A loud annoying buzzer that sounded like a fire alarm punctuated the quiet of the theatre. It was coming from the screen. Ryan looked up to see the words flashing in large red letters: FALSE! FALSE! FALSE!

Chad stood up and walked over to the photos and said, "Well, I guess someone disagrees with you."

"How could I possibly be wrong? That's ridiculous?" Ryan studied the photos intently for another long minute and stroked his forehead with his fingers trying to figure out what he had missed?

"Okay, I am totally confused," he admitted.

"Read the photos again," Chad directed.

Ryan walked over to each of the photos and read the words out loud. "Can't you see, I was joyful, and sad, and angry and all the other emotions you listed here."

"Ryan, you are not unlike most people. It takes time to wrap your head around the concept that explains why the answer is false and not true, as you suggested.

"Tell you what," Chad added, "I'm going to go get us some coffee. You spend some time trying to see if you can figure out why the answer is false. I'll be back soon."

As Chad left the room, Ryan sat down and stared at the photos trying desperately to determine where he had gone wrong. He hated being wrong. Normally, he would go to great lengths to cover up any errors he may have made in anything, rather than feel exposed. Now, not only was he wrong, but he also had no clue as to why.

Before long the theatre door opened but instead of Chad returning with the coffee, again, it was Lance, the last person Ryan wanted to see.

"Hi there Ryan," he said. "I'm done for the day; how about you?"

Ryan's palms started sweating. Just his luck to have the person who didn't think he was ready for an executive position find him sitting dumbfounded.

"Chad had an urgent phone call he had to deal with," Lance said. "He told me you were trying to wrap your head around a new concept and thought you and I might be able to chat about it… I took the Negotiating With Yourself Program a few years ago."

"I didn't know that," Ryan said, a little surprised, "but good luck helping with this one. I've been staring at these photos trying to figure out what I missed and, frankly, I am just drawing a blank. How can the answer possibly be false? Yes, I was sad, I was joyful. Yes, and I was even excited when I came into the theatre for today's session. How can the answer possibly be false?"

"Why don't we get out of here for a change of scenery," Lance suggested. "Sometimes changing the environment helps to re-jig the thinking process."

"What about Chad?" Ryan asked. He really didn't want to spend time with Lance. The last thing he wanted was to have Lance observe him not being able to figure something out.

"I'll send him a text," Lance said.

Ryan followed Lance out into the round room wondering how this might affect Lance's impression of his ability to problem solve. As he watched Lance texting Chad, he realized he was again experiencing Monkey Mind, which led him to realize that every time he interacted with Lance he experienced Monkey Mind. *'One, two, three, redirect!'*

Lance finished the text and put the phone back in his pocket. He was finished for the day so he didn't feel the need to leave his phone in the white box provided in his training area.

As they settled into the circular room, he said to Ryan, "Okay, let's see if this might help you to look at the question in a different light. Remember last year when you called me in a panic because you had to miss an evening meeting because Tara hadn't come home from school and was nowhere to be found? You were frantic, and terrified that something terrible must have happened to her. You had the whole neighbourhood out looking for her. The rest of the team and I came to help look for her.

"I remember when we got to your house you were so frantic and terrified you were yelling at a police officer for standing around because you thought he should have been out looking for Tara. Honestly Ryan, I thought you were going to have a heart attack, given your emotional state.

"An hour later, Tara's cousin pulled into the driveway with Tara in the car. She had seen her walking home and took her to the mall after school. You rushed to the car, opened the door, grabbed Tara and hugged her with tears streaming down your face. So within a minute, you went from terror to anger to relief and then to happiness.

"Now, think about it as if you were an observer watching the whole thing unfold and consider the questions we need to wrap our heads around.

"Was it Ryan who was terrified?

"Were Ryan and his emotion, terror, the same thing, or was it something else, something outside of Ryan that caused him to feel terror?

"Same with joy… is it Ryan that is joyous or is it something outside of Ryan that causes him to feel joy?

"If it is something outside of him, then ask yourself the question again: Ryan was terrified. True or false?"

Ryan hesitated. "Well… I never considered it that way. Can I have a few minutes to think about it?"

"Sure, take as long as you want. If you get it right, Chad said to tell you the deal he made with you is still a go."

"I think I need to take another look at those photos to figure this out."

"Sure," Lance said. "Let's go back then."

Lance followed Ryan back into the theatre. Ryan walked over to the mounted photos.

"I'll just wait here," Lance said as he sat in front of the screen looking up at it as if pondering the question that was left unanswered: "Do you ever think about what you are thinking about?"

Ryan began to pace between the photos and the screen, stopping to look at each. Then he turned to look at the question on the screen and read it out loud.

"Do you ever think about what you are thinking about?"

"Lance!" he suddenly shouted. "I got it, I got it! When I was frantic about Tara I thought she was missing. I thought something terrible had happened to her. Maybe she was kidnapped; maybe she was hit by a car and in the hospital; maybe the bullies at school ganged up on her and hurt her. I was having horrifying thoughts and my Monkey Mind was at play. Then, when I saw her with her cousin, all those thoughts disappeared and were replaced by the one thought that she was safe, and I immediately experienced happiness and relief.

"Lance, I am not my emotions! I have sad thoughts, I have joyous thoughts, I have horrifying thoughts, I even have curious thoughts, but I am not my thoughts! And since my thoughts gave rise to my emotions, I am not my emotions either!

"My thoughts are determined by what is happening outside of me. Tara didn't come home from school so I had horrifying thoughts, but then when I saw her the horror was replaced with thoughts of her being safe. I thought about my father's cancer and I had sad thoughts."

Lance grinned from ear to ear as he stood up and walked over to Ryan. Ryan was so fascinated by his discovery that he had returned to pacing between the photos while talking.

"But the fascinating thing about thoughts is that even though it was two years ago that my father died, the thoughts today caused me to feel sad, even tear up, just as I did two years ago. It seems as if my body was reliving the emotional responses to sad thoughts I had in the past."

"Well," Lance replied, "now there's another fascinating discovery. Even though your thoughts were of the no-longer-existing past, your body was responding as if it was happening now."

At that moment it occurred to Ryan that every time he saw Lance, not only did he experience Monkey Mind, but he relived the anxiety and anger he felt the day he had his performance review. And what a foolish waste of energy and time that was, to invest so heavily in something that was not even real, something in the past.

"Okay Ryan, time to make that decision. Are you coming back tomorrow or is this the end of the program for you?"

Ryan was surprised that he was actually thinking about whether he would come back tomorrow or not. A couple of hours ago he was thrilled at the prospect of this being his last day. He sat down and was silent for a moment. His gaze once again fell on at the life-size photos.

"You know Lance, in spite of my epiphany today, I still don't completely get how happiness and sadness, anger and pain are not part of who we are. Why it's false for me to say, 'Ryan is sad.' But the example you gave makes a lot of sense. I have to say, I'm curious as to what's behind the other doors. I kind of feel like I've discovered a secret or two but and there's another secret to be discovered behind one of those other doors."

"Sounds like you've made your decision. See you tomorrow then?"

"Yes, I'll see you here tomorrow," Ryan replied.

As Lance left the building, Ryan opened the white box and retrieved his phone. He stood for a moment and glanced at the remaining doors, contemplating which he was going to choose for tomorrow.

As he exited the Discovery Centre, he felt a sense of satisfaction, as if he had achieved a victory of some sort but wasn't quite sure what it was. Ryan opened the envelope Chad had left with Lance to give him. It was another card. He read it out loud.

**"You are not your thoughts
Think about what you're thinking about!"**

As he walked across the parking lot, Ryan noticed the flashing red light on his phone. He had messages waiting. He wondered who was trying to reach him and how many things he would have waiting for him at the office. He got into his car and, in an unprecedented move, put the phone in his pocket and decided he wouldn't check messages until he got home.

The ride home was restful and, though Monkey Mind reared its head a few times, Ryan was able to redirect his thoughts to the present and his driving. As he pulled into his driveway he turned the car off and spent the next few minutes going through his e-mail. There was nothing that couldn't wait until tomorrow. With a sense of satisfaction, he turned the phone off and headed into the house.

That evening as Leela prepared dinner Ryan began thinking about some work items he had to complete tomorrow and the meetings he had to arrange with clients, and then the need to clean up the leaves and debris from the eavestroughs invaded his thoughts. The sense of calm he had felt on the way home was quickly being replaced by a low grade sense of anxiety. *'Monkey Mind,'* he thought to himself and, recognizing he was living in the future, he interrupted the thoughts with one, two, three, redirect. He smiled and said out loud to himself, "I guess that was my first muscle workout for the evening."

"What did you say?" Leela called from the kitchen.

"Oh nothing important," he answered, "just mumbling to myself. I'm going up to change. I'll be down in a sec."

Ryan pulled on his sweats and his comfiest T-shirt and headed downstairs. Seizing the present moment, he walked over to help Leela with supper. She glanced at him with a puzzled look as he picked up a tomato and started slicing it.

"Pass me that cucumber Hon," he said as he looked at Leela and smiled.

Leela was curious about Ryan's odd behaviour. She was used to his pattern of going directly upstairs, changing into his sweats and sitting at the dining room table where he would work on his laptop until suppertime. They used to make the salads together years ago, but that was before Tara was born and before he got his present management position.

As he sliced tomatoes, thoughts of the project deadline at work came to Ryan's mind. Was cutting up tomatoes really a good use of his time when he could respond to at least half of his emails by supper. *'One, two, three, redirect'* brought him back to the present moment.

"Quick, open your mouth," he said to Leela as he playfully threw a cherry tomato at her. "Catch!"

Leela reverted to the behaviour of their younger days and opened her mouth, catching the tomato expertly.

"I am still the champ at this game," she gloated, "but what's gotten into you today?"

"Oh nothing," he said. "Just trying out some new techniques I learned at my Negotiating With Yourself Program for thinking about what I'm thinking about."

"Well, whatever they're teaching you, keep practising it. I like it!" she said as she threw an olive at Ryan. "Catch!" To her surprise, he did.

A few minutes later, Ryan opened the patio doors to call his daughter in. "Tara, come in and wash up, it's dinnertime."

"I'm hungry Daddy," she said as she came running. "Are we going to play the taste-your-food game again?"

"Yes we are," he told her, "but today we're going to add a new rule to the game. We have to spend the first five minutes just tasting and enjoying the flavours before we can talk. Deal?"

"Ok," she replied. "I'm setting the egg timer."

The balance of the evening went smoothly, after their playful dinner Ryan decided to do an hour of work and then spend time enjoying a glass of wine with Leela on the patio. While sitting there with her it occurred to him that this was the first time the two of them actually enjoyed the patio set they had purchased the previous summer.

As Ryan hung his sports jacket up at bedtime, the card Chad had left him for him fell out of his pocket. He picked it up and taped it to the bathroom mirror beside the other one and repeated the words on it: "You are not your thoughts. Think about what you're thinking about!"

Chapter 4

Change Your Thoughts Change Your Reality

A minute of clarity is a minute of prosperity

Ryan again awoke to sunshine streaming through his bedroom window. As his feet hit the floor he took a moment to enjoy the feeling of the plush carpet beneath them and take in the rays. He had set his alarm 10 minutes early so as not to be in the usual rush in which everything was timed to the minute, allowing him to head out exactly five minutes before rush hour traffic.

Thoughts of his morning meetings interrupted his enjoyment of the moment. *'Monkey Mind,'* he thought to himself. *'One, two, three, redirect.'* Building his mind muscle seemed like a great way to start the day.

He sat for a few more minutes on the edge of the bed and looked over at Leela as she slept and felt a sense of gratitude for his good fortune.

The ride to work was most unusual. Ryan found himself choosing not to turn on the radio. Instead, he enjoyed the quiet, which seemed to have a calming influence on him.

At 8 a.m. he chose to listen to the morning news for 15 minutes, after which he promptly turned the radio off. As he pulled into the parking lot he thought about how pleasant the ride had been and how relaxed and ready to take on the day he felt.

"Good morning Ashley," Ryan called out to the parking lot attendant.

Ashley looked over at him in surprise. She was used to Ryan walking swiftly past her in a beeline to the front entrance. She was surprised he actually knew her name, although it was on her badge, because he usually rushed by without as much as a glance.

"Good morning Ryan," she replied.

Ryan went into his first meeting feeling unusually calm. He was meeting with a group of managers who had a habit of resisting organizational change. Today's meeting was about implementing a new payroll system.

"Good morning Larry, Anjali, Justin. How are things going?" he asked as he entered the boardroom.

Larry and Anjali looked at each other in surprise. They were used to Ryan starting his meetings by distributing a document outlining his position on the topic at hand.

"Good, how about you?" Larry replied, a little shocked, along with the others, at Ryan's opening remarks.

"Great thanks!" Ryan said with enthusiasm. As he sat down he continued. "So today, I'd like us to take some time and individually clear our minds so we can focus on what we need to accomplish. I know we all have a ton of things that we need to deal with, that's why I now start all my meetings by asking everyone to take the first five minutes and think about what they want to leave the meeting having accomplished."

Larry laughed. "What happened to 'a minute lost is a minute that costs'?"

"Well," said Ryan, "it's been replaced with a minute of clarity is a minute of prosperity. So shall we begin? Think about what you hope to get out of this meeting."

Ryan looked down at his watch, proud and happy to be wearing it instead of relying on his cell phone for everything.

The first couple of minutes of silence were awkward for Larry and Anjali. They looked at each other puzzled, or simply gazed around the room. Justin seemed to be enjoying the think time while Anjali took out a pen and started jotting down a few outcomes she wanted from the meeting. Larry saw what she was doing and also started to think about what he wanted to get out of the meeting.

"Okay, five minutes are up," Ryan pronounced. "Shall we begin?"

Anjali spoke first. "I want to understand why we have to change to this new payroll system in the first place. The old one seems to me to be working very well."

"Okay, how about if we put that under New Business and discuss it after we move through the agenda," Ryan suggested.

The meeting progressed well. Ryan made sure to address Anjali's's concerns, along with those of the others present. An hour later he ended the meeting with a feeling of success. Justin and Anjali seemed more conducive to implementing the new system, and Ryan better understood that their resistance had been more than just resistance to change. They had some legitimate concerns that needed to be addressed.

With an hour before his next appointment with his new employee, Anaka, Ryan started ruminating about the last time he interacted with her. She had accused him of being sexist, saying that he was giving all the complex and desirable projects to Dave and leaving her with busy work. He was determined to show her that he had confidence in her abilities by assigning her to a new project, but without hard time lines.

As he waited for Anaka to arrive, Ryan felt himself having negative thoughts. He knew he should stop and could hear a whisper in the back of his mind trying to break through. *'Monkey Mind. Monkey Mind... Monkey Mind.'* But he ignored it and continued to replay the conversation from his last meeting with Anaka, ruminating on his explanation to her about why he had given Larry the complex project.

He would explain again that he had considered her but she just did not have the experience. He felt his stomach tighten and his palms start to sweat. He couldn't seem to stop himself from pondering and reliving his last meeting with her over and over, which was finally interrupted by knocking at his office door.

As she came in, Anaka had an unfriendly look about her. Ryan recognized it as the kind of negativity you can sometimes feel in your gut before someone even says anything. He found himself on autopilot, going on the defensive. He didn't intend to do that but there was something about Anaka's unfriendly presence—the way she aggressively pulled out the chair to sit down, the way she folded her arms when she sat down—it all hit a nerve in him.

"Hi Anaka," he said, trying to be friendly. "How's your day going so far?"

"Fine," came her terse response as she gazed out the office window, purposely avoiding eye contact with Ryan.

"Well that's good," he said. "Today I wanted to follow up on our last meeting. I know you left a bit upset so I thought we should bring some closure to the issue we were discussing."

"That fine," she said. "I'm fine with your decision. I really don't need to discuss it any further."

Ryan felt his palms sweating and his stomach tightening up. "Anaka, as your supervisor it's my job to tell you where improvements can be made. That's what I was trying to do at our last meeting, trying to explain to you that I gave Dave the Hydro project because he has more experience with that type of project, and we are on a very tight deadline. But you didn't seem satisfied with that explanation so I want to discuss why you think it was sexist."

Anaka couldn't believe that Ryan was speaking to her in such an aggressive manner. She was determined to keep her cool and continue to say she was fine with his decision, even though she still believed it was sexist.

"Look, I said I was fine with it," she insisted. "There's really no need to continue to discuss something that's already been decided." She continued to gaze out the window with only an occasional glance at Ryan.

"But there is a need Anaka. I can't have you going around telling people that I'm sexist. I'm not, and you need to understand that you are not doing yourself any good by accusing me of being sexist. Everyone around here knows that I am the last person to treat women differently. You need to understand that."

Anaka was getting visibly upset at Ryan's insistence that they revisit the last meeting. Her neck was red and blotchy and she could feel her face getting warm.

"I'm sorry," she said. "I have to excuse myself." She got up and walked out the door.

Ryan was stunned. He sat motionless wondering why she left so abruptly.

When the initial shock wore off, he found his mind spitting out angry thoughts.

'How dare she walk out on the meeting! Who does she think she is? She has only been with the company for four months. She doesn't determine what we discuss, that's the problem with this generation Y.'

On and on he went, getting angrier by the minute. *'Monkey Mind, Monkey Mind!'* Ryan knew his thoughts were controlling him. He knew he was on autopilot. He desperately tried to redirect. *'One, two, there, breathe, redirect.'* But it didn't work! Monkey Mind was in control.

With the meeting cut short Ryan had an extra 45 minutes before leaving for the Discovery Centre. He pulled out his priority file and tried to work on a project plan but instead he continued to agonize about Anaka until his thoughts were interrupted by a knock at the door.

"Come in," he said, somewhat annoyed.

"Hi," Lance said. "Do you have a minute?"

'How does he have this uncanny ability to show up at the worst times?' Ryan asked himself.

"Sure, come on in," he said.

"So how has your morning been?" Lance asked with an air of hesitation.

"Do you want the template answer, or the truth?"

"Well, respectful honesty would be my preference," he replied.

"Well then, it started off great. My meeting with Larry, Justin, and Anjali went great but then… Well, my meeting with Anaka was a bust. I don't know how I went from great to what feels likes failure."

"I know," Lance said. "Anaka came to see me."

"She came to see you? Really! What did she say?"

"Well, she felt somewhat bullied, but I'm more interested in what you think shifted the meeting to the point of her leaving. You said the meeting with her felt like a failure. I personally hate to use the word failure, but if you see it that way, then also see that every so-called failure is a growth opportunity. You know the old saying about turning lemons into lemonade."

Ryan snickered "Ya, right… I wish."

"Well, how about this? I'm prepared to bet you that whatever you consider a failure can be turned into an opportunity."

Lance was the last person Ryan wanted to talk to about Anaka. His thoughts shifted around to the executive position that was open and how Anaka's visit to Lance would seal his fate. There was no way now that Lance would recommend him for any executive position.

"I really doubt this can be turned into an opportunity," he said, "but okay, let me tell you my side of the story."

Ryan explained how Anaka had previously accused him of being sexist, and how he had gone into the meeting with the intention of offering her the opportunity to work on a new upcoming, more complex project. But she came into the office intending to be difficult, folding her arms and responding to him with curt one-word answers, looking out the window, etc. Instead of offering her the new project, he found himself giving her an explanation of why he was not sexist, and what his role was as her supervisor, and how, despite his attempts to avoid her thinking him sexist by explaining his role at the beginning, she just up and walked out on him.

Lance scratched his chin.

"Hmmm… interesting. Tell me, what were you thinking about before Anaka arrived at your door."

"Lots of things… I was thinking about the last meeting and how badly it went, how I didn't want a repeat of the same thing, how unfair she was at the last meeting, not to mention rude and not prepared to listen to anything I had to say. But I was also thinking that I need to have a good working relationship with her so I was going to assign her to the new Sandman Project. It's complex and a priority for the company."

"You didn't get a chance to tell her about Sandman? You got thrown off by what you saw as her unfriendly demeanour?"

"Exactly… she folded her arms, angrily pulled her chair out before sitting, and had a really unfriendly look about her."

"Ryan, have you ever heard about emotional contagion?"

"Emotional what?"

"Contagion."

"Nope… never heard of it?"

"Well, no better time than the present to learn," Lance said, and then went on. "What door were you going to choose for today's session at the training centre?"

"It was going to be a toss-up between Who Hijacked My Emotions, and Today Is the First Day of the Rest of Your Life. I know, I know, I let Monkey Mind get the better of me. Believe me, I thought about that after she left but I just couldn't pull myself out of it. I tried to interrupt my thoughts and redirect to the present but I guess I was just too angry regurgitating what happened at the last meeting. In fact, I probably spent a lot of time in the last two weeks reliving it over and over. Yes, I was definitely living in the past."

"Well don't be too hard on yourself. Remember, most of us have been controlled by our thoughts all our lives. It's going to take more than two afternoons to undo lifelong patterns. The important thing is to acknowledge that you've been living much of your life on autopilot because you can't change what you don't acknowledge."

Lance then looked at his watch and abruptly said, "We can talk later but I have to head out now. I'm looking forward to my own discoveries this afternoon."

Chapter 5

Who Hijacked My Emotions?

*Claim your power
To choose your reaction*

As Ryan walked through the doors of the Discovery Centre he felt a tinge of regret recognizing that he had spent the entire drive there ruminating over the situation with Anaka. He stepped out of the car determined not to let Monkey Mind get the better of him.

The sight of the lilac bushes reminded him of the need to enjoy the present moment. He took a moment to breathe in their sweet fragrance as he walked toward the door, and to feel the warmth of the sun on his back.

He entered the circular room and went directly to the white box and placed his phone in it. Already feeling a sense of calm, he exhaled as he locked the box. He sunk into the white chair, enjoying the comfort of the familiar soft leather. *'Fifteen minutes of restful contemplation,'* he thought to himself and closed his eyes, determined to clear his mind and prepare for the afternoon session.

Fifteen minutes later, after just five redirecting, the voice on the intercom came on gently inviting him to choose a door. He got up and entered the Who Hijacked My Emotions door?

This room was different from all the others. It appeared to be a small office space with a comfy sofa, a matching chair, and a coffee table in the middle.

Ryan sat on the sofa and looked around the room. There was an abstract pastel green and yellow painting on one wall and a certificate of some sort on another. He squinted to read the certificate but still couldn't make it out. Before he could get up to get a closer view, Chad walked in.

"Hi Ryan, how are you doing today?"

"Not that great," he said, "but I'm managing. What do you have in store for me today? Am I getting hijacked?"

Chad laughed as he said, "Well, no... today we are just going to have a chat and work through some of your feelings about your workplace, and Anaka."

"How do you know about Anaka?"

"Lance told me about your incident. He thought it would do you good to talk about it."

"Gee, what is this, the proverbial psychiatrist chair?"

"Actually Ryan, I am a psychologist," Chad said, pointing to the certificate on the wall.

"Did Lance set you up to do this? Is this part of his strategy?"

"What strategy is that Ryan?"

"Never mind," he said, not wanting to dwell on Lance's role in the executive search.

"Well, we have an hour together so let's see what you can discover in that time. Are you willing to learn something that will help you to be more effective the next time you meet with Anaka?"

"I do have another meeting with her tomorrow, so why not? According to her, I'm just a sexist bully."

"Okay, let's start by reviewing how your morning started. How were you feeling when you went to work this morning?"

"Good, until I had my meeting with Anaka."

"So it sounds like something happened to change your mood from positive to negative. What was it?"

"Well it wasn't anything specific that she said. It was more the way she was so aggressive... just plain unfriendly, like someone expecting a battle."

"So how did you respond to that?"

"Well, I guess I put my fighting gloves on as well, even though I had the opposite intention. I wanted to offer her an olive branch."

"Well, I think if we examine what actually happened you will find the secret that will turn that lemon into lemonade."

"What secret… that I put my fighting gloves on?"

"No, the knowledge that someone can hijack your emotions, intentionally or unintentionally, and you would never know it. Have you ever heard about emotional contagion?"

"I think Lance mentioned it this morning. He said I would learn about it here."

"And so you will," Chad reassured him. "There's been lots of research done in this area. And that research will reveal to you something that will serve you well for the rest of your life. In fact, if others are not aware of it, it will give you the upper hand in difficult situations."

"Okay then," Ryan said, "I'm all ears for anything that will give me the upper hand."

"Well, research tells us that when we are feeling angry or sad, happy or glad, we can communicate negative or positive emotions to the people with whom we are interacting. It suggests that in a group, a single person's mood can significantly influence the mood of others in the group. So imagine what that means for your whole department, or any team of people working together."

"Ya, I can see how that could be a secret weapon, especially if you're the only one in the group that knows what's happening… but what about with just individuals. If you're with a single person who is exhibiting negative emotions, like Anaka, can that person affect you in the same way as in a group?"

"Yes, certainly!" Chad said enthusiastically. "It's fascinating to look at all the neuroscience research available and what it's telling us. For example, we now know that if you think about a particular emotional experience you have had, and sympathize with it, the same brain circuits that fire when you were actually having that experience become activated."

"So that would mean that when I am thinking about how angry Anaka had made me the first time," Ryan said, "the same brain circuits fire as if I am really angry with her in the present moment, even though she's not even there."

"Yes, and that can affect your body. If you start sympathizing with the emotional experience, you might find yourself exhibiting similar body reactions, like tightening in your stomach, or increased heart rate. So it's like you are reliving the experience physically as well."

"Now that you mention it, I intended to make things better but I did spend time before the meeting thinking about how rude and disrespectful she had been in the previous meeting… and maybe she also spent her time before the meeting working herself up about how I was unfair and sexist."

"And that's a lot of toxic emotions percolating in one room at the same time," Chad said. "A breeding ground for emotional contagion, I would say. That's why it's so important that as a manager you be aware of the mood you are in, or your emotions may set the tone for the meeting before you even open your mouth.

"You know how you hear people talking about someone having negative energy? I think it's really emotional contagion they're talking about. It's not only important to know how you might be affecting others but equally important to know how other people's toxic emotions might be affecting you."

"Now that you mention it," Ryan said, "there are always some departments where whenever you walk into them you can feel the anxiety and stress… and then there are those where everyone always seems to be happy and content and willing to provide support with whatever is needed."

"You know Ryan, I've met people who purposefully use emotional contagion to get their way in negotiations. They walk in exuding a certain aura or attitude, like 'I'm going to be difficult to get along with,' and their unsuspecting victim gets his or her emotions hijacked. Then there are those who unarm their opponents by oozing with positivity. In that situation the result can be that win/win becomes the aim for all present. But it's more complex than just the transfer of emotions."

"Ya, I know, I was just thinking about my conversation with Lance. I agreed that I was not my emotions, and my emotions are based on what my thoughts are. I also agreed that I'm not my thoughts."

"Good, I am impressed with your summary of the Thinking About What You're Thinking About session. But let me add to that summary that your thoughts can also hijack your body."

"Lots of hijacking going on around here," Ryan quipped.

"For sure," Chad said. "To understand how powerful our thoughts are, consider this: Many people, when embarrassed or angry, turn red in the face. And we know that embarrassment and anger are caused by what people are thinking about. But what you don't see is your sympathetic nervous system responding to what it perceives as a threat. It could be an emotional threat or a physical threat. When that happens, the system becomes overactive and triggers the expansion of the blood vessels that run close to the surface of the skin. The expansion allows more blood to flow, which causes your face to turn red.

"Basically, your body is preparing you for a fight or flight. So when you recognize physical sensations, like your face getting warm, or your stomach tightening, stop and think about what you are thinking about because it is those thoughts that may be causing the discomfort you are feeling.

"When you consciously think about what you are thinking, you interrupt the thought, and when you interrupt the thought you can interrupt the emotion. When you interrupt the emotion you can interrupt the physical sensations. Magic! Right?"

"Hmmm," Ryan mused as Chad continued.

"When you are meeting with a difficult person or feel yourself feeling uncomfortable with a situation, or you are annoyed, one way to interrupt all of that is to do a body scan."

"A what?"

"A body scan. It's kind of like checking the weather forecast, except the weather is you. Are you feeling stormy, gloomy, foggy, or sunny? Here, now we can do the proverbial psychiatrist couch. You can do this on your own sitting or lying down, depending where you are. Since we have a sofa here, relax, lie down."

"Okay, but don't be offended if I fall asleep."

"Oh you won't," Chad assured him. "So, basically, you want to notice and be aware of any discomfort you may be feeling—warmth, tension, sweaty palms, tightness in your stomach, stiffness in your neck."

"I can do it sitting in my office if I want?"

"You sure can. In fact, once you've done it a few times you can do in a couple of minutes… like before a meeting, you just do a quick weather check."

"Okay, so how do I do that?"

"Start by focusing on your feet and slowly let your attention drift up to your lower legs, then your upper legs, slowly moving up to your abdomen, your chest, your neck, jaw and head, noticing any discomfort you might feel anywhere along the way. If you feel tightness or sweaty palms, for example, just be aware of it. At minimum, you will be aware that you are feeling physical discomfort and your thoughts may be affecting you in a negative way, which can be pretty valuable knowledge before you go into a meeting."

A body scan is also a great tool to interrupt your thoughts. If you are having negative or unproductive thoughts, if you're ruminating about something, you can interrupt those thoughts by doing a body scan."

A knock at the door interrupted Chad's weather lesson.

"Hey, how's it going?" Lance asked as he entered. "I'm done for the day; what about you?"

Chad turned to Ryan. "What do you think? Are we done for the day?"

"I'll need some time to absorb all this new information but, yes, I think so."

"Well, I think I've done enough teaching for one day too, so Lance, why don't you do the walk with Ryan? It's the next tool in the box for interrupting a thought."

"Sure, would love to," Lance replied. "Ryan, you ready for some sunshine? We're going for a walk."

Ryan hesitated, he would prefer not to spend the rest of the afternoon with Lance but he didn't want to offend him.

"Sure," he said. "But what about your workshop?"

"Oh no problem there, as part of our homework we have to teach someone a new concept they can use daily at work, so this is perfect."

A warm breeze was blowing and the sun was shining. It was a beautiful day for a walk. Ryan brushed past the lilac bushes as Lance began walking toward the open green space beyond the parking lot. Ryan followed.

As they moved along Ryan increased his pace, moving slightly ahead of Lance.

"Where's the fire?" Lance asked.

"Oh, sorry. I guess I'm just used to walking fast," Ryan responded with a tinge of embarrassment.

"Well, no fires are burning today," Lance said. "I'm going to teach you how to walk in magic. As a wise 98-year-old man once told me, 'Lance, your body is your best friend.' And how right he was because this next tool requires the use of your body."

"I know walking can interrupt our thoughts," Ryan said, anticipating the lesson. "I do that when I have a problem that I can't solve. I go for a walk and hash it out in my head, then come back to my desk and write out my options."

"No Ryan," Lance told him. "Actually, this will be the opposite of that. In fact, you need to clear your mind of all thoughts and focus on the act of walking. Some call it mindful walking.

"Here, let me show you. While you're walking I want you to feel your body weight pushing toward the ground. Pay particular attention to the heel-to-toe motion."

As he demonstrated and then watched Ryan, he asked "Can you feel it?"

"Ya... I can do the heel to toe thing, no problem. Now what."

"That's really all I want you to focus on, that heel-to-toe motion. Believe me, you're going to be distracted by thoughts. Let's face it, focusing on our foot motion is about as exciting as watching molasses flow, but trust me, it's another good tool for interrupting your thoughts and building your mind muscle. Now let's do it for an entire 15 minutes. When you get distracted by your thoughts, refocus on your heel-to-toe motion."

"Seriously?" Ryan asked. "That's it? Just pay attention to my foot hitting the ground and the heel-to-toe motion for the entire walk?"

"Well, yes, pretty much. You can do this walking to and from the parking lot or to and from meetings. Once you have mastered the focused attention on the motion if you are outside on a quiet street or among trees and greenery, you can also enjoy the smells, sounds and the view. This will help you to be in the present moment and keep Monkey Mind away."

Ryan recalled a study he recently read having to do with walking. "Did you hear about the study about walking in nature," he asked Lance. "They say that a walk through nature, say a park, helps people reduce rumination and also shows reduced neural activity in the area of the brain linked to risk for mental illness."

"No," Lance replied, "I didn't hear about that but it sounds fascinating. Here's the thing, instead of taking your problem with you on your walk, once your walk is finished, you will likely be more focused and able to consider more creative and effective solutions to your problem. Walking through nature actually reduces stress."

"So really, the heel-to-toe focus is the same as when you focus on your breath. It basically shifts your thinking from autopilot to your being in control and in the present?"

"Yes, you got it," Lance agreed as he looked down at his watch. "Oh shoot! I have to pick up my son. We spent so much time talking we didn't get to much walking so that will be your homework tonight and tomorrow. Still, I taught you something, so my homework is done. Now for your homework, find a way to build present moment walking into your day. I want you do a walk for at least 10 minutes tonight, and also make a list of all the opportunities you have for walking. Remember, there's no one recipe so be creative in finding ways to make this a natural part of your day… not an add-on."

Ryan agreed to the homework and then went back into the building to get his phone while Lance headed for the parking lot. He opened the box to find a plasticized card with the quotation: "Claim Your Power to Choose Your Reaction."

He then left the building, got into his car and started the drive home. Within a few moments he turned on the radio. The music seemed different somehow, distracting and noisier than usual. Realizing he was living in autopilot, he turned it off again and before he knew it he was pulling into his driveway.

He spent a few minutes in the car reviewing his emails and quickly responded to an urgent matter, then took some time to consider what he wanted to accomplish that evening. He decided he mostly wanted to spend some quality time with Leela.

He liked this idea of checking his emails in the car and putting his phone away for a while once he got home, especially after hearing about the addictive nature of technology. He intentionally asked himself what he wanted to accomplish in the evening to avoid being on autopilot. This would become his new ritual when he arrived home.

"Yum, something smells good," he announced as he entered the kitchen. Must be my favourite... pasta."

Leela smiled, remembering how Ryan would never order pasta at restaurants, claiming that after eating her pasta, restaurant pasta could never satisfy his taste buds. She hadn't heard him say that for a long time. Instead, much of their restaurant conversation revolved around "need to do" stuff. Need to... replace the windows... find a plumber... do our taxes... It seemed like they hadn't had a relaxing night out in years.

Ryan went over and gave Leela a hug from behind, "Yum, my mouth is watering," he said.

"I still have the salad to do," she replied, hoping he might continue to do some of the things they had enjoyed in their younger days when money was tight and all they had for entertainment was each other.

"Well let me help you," he said. "Let's see, cherry tomatoes... lettuce... Where is the goat cheese?"

"Behind the yogurt," she said.

As he tore the romaine leaves Ryan wondered about how he could fix things at work with Anaka and felt himself getting anxious. *Monkey Mind,* he thought. *'One, two, three, redirect.'*
He refocused on tearing the lettuce, paying attention to the colour and texture, even noticing it seemed crisper than usual. As he started slicing the tomatoes he became aware of Leela's presence near him and realized he had missed this simple family togetherness. But she had been there every day! It was him who had been on autopilot and not living in the present. He finished the salad and they sat down to eat. Tara was at a friend's till bedtime so they had the house to themselves. As they began to eat they both spent a few minutes experiencing the sight, taste and smells of the food.

"Hey Leela, remember how we always used to like going for quiet walks in the park after dinner?"

"Ya, those were the good old days weren't they."

"Well why don't we make it part of today, with a little twist I just learned?"

"I'd love to, but a walking technique? That's a new one for me... But wait a minute, I thought you would be working so I was going to meet Nora for coffee…" She paused a moment but as their eyes met, she added, "But it's okay, she won't mind if I reschedule."

After supper Leela and Ryan ventured out to a nearby park. The air was warm, and the scent of freshly cut grass was a welcome change.

"Okay," he said as they got out of the car, "before we start, let me explain the two simple rules to this technique. Rule number one is there's no talking. We can walk together but we can't talk."

Leela smiled and placed her hand in Ryan's. "Can we hold hands?" she asked with a smile.

Ryan was not really sure if walking with someone else was actually okay, let alone holding hands, but he recalled Lance telling him there was no single recipe so he took some liberty.

"Sure, we can hold hands," he said, "but you have to follow the second rule as well."

"And what might that be?" Leela asked, secretly enjoying the fact that Ryan was trying to teach her a technique for walking.

"Rule two is that your senses—sight, sound, smell, touch—are totally active in paying attention to the experience of walking."

Leela giggled. "So you can enjoy the smell of my new perfume and the sight of me walking, the touch of my hand maybe?"

Ryan gently placed her hand in his, "Yes I can, and while I'm doing that, you can feel the heel-to-toe motion of your feet on the grass, breathe in the fresh air, and notice how it feels in your lungs. And enjoy the smell of the flowers. How does that sound?"

"Anything that gets me outside and around nature sounds good to me," Leela said as she took off her sandals. "Can I take off my shoes and feel the movement of my feet on this luscious green grass?"

"Yes, as long as you stay present on the experience. Don't go off thinking about vacation planning in the lush greenery of the Caribbean, or something like that."

"And if I do end up planning my next vacation, then what?"

"Then you just take three deep breaths, feel the air going into your lungs, and refocus on your heel-to-toe motion."

Leela smiled and gave Ryan a peck on the cheek. "Now I've seen everything," she said. "I never dreamed the day would come when you, my darling, would be teaching me about a walking meditation. You know I read about this in a meditation journal a while ago?"

Ryan saw a twinkle in Leela's eye that had been missing for a very long time, or maybe he had just failed to notice it. He remembered when they were dating, he would tease her about the mischievous twinkle in her eyes reflecting the meaning of the name Leela, which meant divine play.

The walk was more calming than Ryan imagined it would be. He found himself feeling more energetic and alive than he had in a long time. But then again, he hadn't walked in nature, or with Leela since his birthday eight months ago.

After their walk, instead of driving over to pick Tara up from her friend's house, which was a short distance away, Ryan decided he would walk to get her and, as Leela called it, do his walking meditation. On the way home he taught Tara the new walking game as well and they practised all the way home.

Tara won the game because she had less Monkey Mind than Ryan did. The walk was more difficult for him than he had expected because his thoughts kept wandering to Anaka. Every time his mind would stubbornly distract him from the present he would redirect it with a smile, reminding himself that not only was he getting a physical workout, but he was also exercising his mind muscle.

Chapter 6

Divine Play

"Our own worst enemies cannot harm us as much as unwise thoughts."
Buddha

The sun streamed through the bedroom window to greet Ryan the next morning as he awoke. He was feeling particularly energetic and bounced out of bed, his feet sinking into the plush carpet. He smiled as he took a moment to look at Leela still asleep on her side of the bed.

He then stood at the window admiring the blue spruce he and Leela had planted the year they moved into the house. It was no more than three feet tall then but now it was at least eight feet high. Ryan realized he hadn't noticed in a long time just how tall it had grown and how beautiful it was. He wondered how much more he had missed over the years.

He scanned the tiger lilies that Leela had planted on her own because he was busy that particular weekend. In fact, she and Tara had done a lot of the gardening themselves recently.

He noticed a squirrel scurrying up a tree and was surprised to see a statue of a boy and girl holding hands beside the rose bush. He soaked it all in before continuing his morning routine, even managing to get through it all with less Monkey Mind than usual. He took pride in bringing his attention back to the present moment quickly and more easily than before.

Ryan decided to have his coffee outdoors on the patio and savoured every mouthful while enjoying the smell of the crisp morning air, and admiring the tiger lilies. He never thought mornings could be something to look forward to, but this experience was one he decided he wanted to repeat for many mornings to come.

The ride to work had an aura of peacefulness about it. The ongoing "mental traffic" in Ryan's head had lessened, resulting in a sense of calm throughout his body. Whether it was because he decided not to turn the radio on that morning, or simply not being on autopilot, he didn't care. All he knew was that he liked the feeling.

As he entered the parking lot at work, he remembered Anaka and the blow up with her. Monkey Mind had taken control and off he went. He started to worry, recalling her storming out of the office. What would his next step be? He needed a strategy for his 11 o'clock meeting with her. His anxiety-inducing self-talk continued as he walked through the parking lot.

"Good morning," someone said. "Ryan looked up to see a cheerful Ashley waving at him as he realized Monkey Mind had already taken over his peaceful morning.

"Oh, Hi," he replied. "Good morning."

"Gosh, how stupid am I trying to work out a strategy in the parking lot,' he thought to himself. *'One, two, three, redirect.'*

He refocused on the sights and sounds of his immediate environment. This was a good time to do a bit of mindful walking. In fact, he would write it on his list as one of his daily rituals. As he entered the building he was determined to put Anaka out of his thoughts until he decided it was time to think about her.

He recalled Leela telling Tara to put her problem in an imaginary box in her head, put the box on a shelf and they would plan a time to open the box and talk about it. It always worked for Tara. She would stop talking about whatever was on her mind and Leela would get back to her later to discuss it.

Ryan wondered if it might work for him. It was, after all, the same principal of interrupting a thought that's consuming you. He visualized an imaginary file in his head, labelled it Anaka, and decided to figure out his strategy after his first morning meeting.

"Hi Ryan," Rachel said as Ryan approached.

"Good morning Rachel. How are things this morning?"

"Going great," she replied. "I finished my Power Point so I'm all set for today's meeting."

"Great! Looking forward to your presentation."

Ryan entered the boardroom for his 9 o'clock team meeting with positive anticipation. "Okay folks," he said, "let's take five minutes to clear our minds so we can focus on today's agenda… and think about what you want to get out of today's meeting."

The first two agenda items were dealt with quickly and efficiently. Rachel's presentation was next and, at one point, Ryan found himself drifting to thoughts of Anaka. He used one-two-three-redirect and reminded himself that the file would be reviewed after the meeting he was currently at, not during it! Leela's idea of putting issues in a box until it was time to deal with them was working well.

Finally, it was time, 10 a.m. and he could prepare for his meeting with Anaka. He was seated at his office desk reliving the last meeting with her. Sensing his own anxiety, he decided to do a body scan before pulling the file. He started at his feet, slowly moving up his body. All was well until he got to his stomach and felt uneasiness there, a tightness that was uncomfortable. He recognized it as the way he felt whenever he had to go into a meeting he was dreading.

As he continued up his body he noticed that his neck, too, felt tight. He recognized that as what often happened when he had to deal with something unpleasant. He took a few deep breaths and tried to relax.

He was not in the best state to actually deal with Anaka and Ryan knew it. Yet, he was determined to find a solution that would be satisfactory to both of them. He momentarily wondered if it was possible that Anaka was right, and he was a little hasty in his decision. He did after all immediately give the client Dave's name without giving it a second thought. He took out a blank piece of paper and jotted down some statements about the outcomes he wanted from their meeting:

'Her knowing that I respect her work and her abilities

'Her feeling confident that she added value to the team

'Her accepting training to help build her skills in areas where she had little experience'

With the outcomes he wanted in mind, Ryan went about developing a strategy. Before long it was 11 a.m. and Anaka was at the door. She entered his office as she had last time, with a scowl on her face. Ryan recognized the danger of his emotions being hijacked and greeted her with a sincere smile, feeling confident he would be able to help her see his true intent.

"Thanks for coming," he began. "I really want to talk about how I can support you in meeting your career goals."

"Well," she replied with scepticism, "I don't think you even really know my goals... one was to be lead on the project you gave Dave."

"We can come back to that," Ryan replied, "but let's talk about what you want for yourself long term, not just short-term. I'm really interested in your long-term goals, where you see yourself five years from now."

I haven't really thought about five years from now," she said, "but, I guess if I had to think about it, I would say I would want to be in a management position of some sort."

As the meeting progressed, Anaka began to soften her tone and listen more openly to what Ryan had to say. She began to open up about the kind of training needs she felt she could benefit from and, lo and behold, the synergy of their ideas created an opportunity for Anaka that was evident to Ryan.

"You know, Anaka," he told her, "I think your long-term goal for management is quite realistic. In fact, I am wondering if you have heard about our mentorship program."

"No," she said. "Since I'm new here I'm still trying to get a handle on a lot of things."

"Well," Ryan said, "I'm one of the mentors in that program and many of the skills you want to develop are things I can help you with. If you would like, I could make a recommendation to Human Resources that you be enrolled in the program… and I would be happy to be your mentor."

"Really? You would do that for me? she asked. "That would be great."

"Consider it done then. I will send an email to HR today. They will give you a call to come in and fill out the program application and we can start next month."

Anaka left Ryan's office with a smile on her face, which greatly pleased Ryan. He closed his door, sunk back into his chair, ignored the flashing light on his cell phone, and enjoyed the moment. Before he knew it, it was time to leave for his last session at the Discovery Centre.

As he walked to the parking lot, he hummed one of his favourite tunes, *Rise Up* by Andra Day. He smiled when he got to the line, "and we can walk it out." He was still in awe of what had happened with Anaka when he remembered he had to submit a list to Lance of opportunities to practise mindful walking.

With great difficulty, he interrupted his thoughts and redirected his senses to his environment and the heel-to-toe movement of his feet on the pavement. As he scanned the area, to his delight he noticed a 1956 Chevy Bel Air in the lot.

"Hey, nice car," he said to the woman about to get in it. "I haven't seen one of these since my grandfather had his."

"It's part of my antique car collection," the woman said. "I've been driving this one to work for the past month."

"Really, I'm surprised I haven't seen it here before today," Ryan said. "I love antique cars. In fact, I have a collection of photos of antique cars that I've been collecting since I was a teenager."

"Well," the woman replied, "how would you like to be my guest at the upcoming antique road show? It's coming into town in a few months. In fact, I'm one of the co-ordinators for the city."

"That would be great," Ryan responded with excitement. "Someone told me there was a road show coming to town but I didn't get much more information than that. Here's my card," she said as she reached into her jacket pocket. "Please do give me a shout. I would love to see your collection sometime."

"Absolutely! I love to show off my collection."

As Ryan got into his car he realized how much more there was to work than meetings and paperwork. It seems he had forgotten about the "people first" part.

As he arrived at the Discovery Centre, he reminded himself to focus on the sights, smells and sounds. He felt the warm sun on his back, noticed a bird's nest in a nearby tree, heard children playing in the nearby park, and spent a moment enjoying the lilacs.

"So, do you have that list for me?" Lance asked as he greeted Ryan just inside the front door.

For the first time in a long time, Ryan was happy to see Lance. "Lance, you won't believe what happened today!"

"Really, what happened?"

"Remember I told you about Anaka and how my last meeting with her was a dismal failure?"

"Yes," he said. "She's the new employee who accused you of being sexist, right?

"Ya... well today I used the tools I learned here, including recognizing emotional contagion, and it was like magic! Seriously, our meeting went better than I could ever have imagined. In fact, I'm going to be her mentor. Can you believe it?"

"Well, I'm not surprised. Recognizing emotional contagion is a powerful tool. Hard to imagine most people carry on in life without ever knowing they have the ability to influence the mood and emotions of others, or that others have the power to influence theirs. It seems you are really having a positive impact on your team Ryan. You're becoming quite the change agent."

"I am?" Ryan said, puzzled at Lance's comment. Lance was the last person he expected to refer to him as a change agent, especially after his last performance appraisal, but he was determined not to live in the past.

"Most definitely!" Lance said. "Today I was at a meeting of one of your team members and he started by asking everyone to take a few minutes to transition from their last meeting and spend some time thinking about what they wanted to get out of the current one. When I complimented him on the idea, he said it was your new ritual for starting staff meetings. And since he found it helpful, he now starts all his own meetings that way."

After a pause, he went on. "When small things start to influence others, over time they can change the whole organizational culture. Trust me," he said emphatically, "I have seen organizations go from mistrust and hostility toward their leadership to a welcoming and trusting culture. The change agent came from a few leaders practising small steps that had an impact on others to do the same. Before you know it, you are changing the way people work and think and behave and treat each other… the whole blueprint behind their workplace environment and culture changes."

"I can see that now," Ryan said. "And thank you for that but, speaking of blueprints for change, here's my list for building walking into my day."

Ryan entered the circular room with a sense of excitement. He could never have imagined he would be excited to attend this program. He immediately put his phone in the white box, feeling a sense of relief to be able to get rid of it for a time. Today, the last day of the program, he would learn the fourth and final secret.

Lance sat in the white leather chair and read Ryan's list. "It sounds like you did your homework, and more," he said. "I especially like your walk with Tara. She's going to be one brilliant kid if you start teaching her at this age to train her Monkey Mind."

Ryan laughed. "It was the only way I would get any peace and quiet walking home with her."

"Now," Lance added, "the question is, can you build any of this into your daily routine and make it a habit? Remember, you can do this indoors as well. What is important is to shut out the mental traffic.

"Well," Ryan said, "the parking lot to the office would be an easy one because I have to be there every day, twice a day. And I would love to be able to go for a walk with Leela after supper in the evenings, but that's not always practical."

"Why not?"

"Because we need someone there to take care of Tara."

"Why not take her with you?" Lance asked. "You've already taught her how to do it."

"But can I do that," Ryan wondered out loud. "...have the whole family walking with me?"

"Hey, as I said, there is no one recipe. Do what works for your lifestyle. Be creative, as long as you follow the basic principles of focused attention."

"Okay then," Ryan said, reassured. "That's great... I read somewhere that it takes 90 days to develop a new habit, so come and talk to me in three months and I'll tell you how it went."

Suddenly the intercom interrupted them. "Please spend the next 15 minutes relaxing and preparing your mind for this afternoon's session."

Lance left and Ryan sunk into the comfy leather chair, closed his eyes, and let himself drift into silence. He was so relaxed that his usual relief at hearing the intercom voice tell him his 15 minutes was over was replaced with disappointment.

"It's time to pick the lucky door for your last day with us?" the voice continued.

He picked Today is the First Day of The Rest of Your Life.

Chapter 7

Thoughts are Just Thoughts Thoughts are Not Facts

"Today is the first day of the rest of your life."
Charles Dederich

Live it!

Ryan stepped through the door and was shocked to see a room full of people seated at round tables. The tables were covered with pristine white table cloths with orange bird-of-paradise centrepieces. The lights were low, creating an aura of some kind of dinner event.

Chad greeted him at the entrance before Ryan had time to take it all in and lead Ryan to a table close to the front of the room. He was seated with a middle-aged man in a tan coloured suit and a thirty-something woman in a black suit. Chad sat beside Ryan.

The lights dimmed even more and focused on the stage where the presenter was about to enter. As he was fruitlessly trying to distinguish the faces of others in the room, Ryan felt a tap on his shoulder from behind him.

"Lance, what are you doing here? And where did all these people come from."

"They're all previous participants from the Negotiating with Yourself Program," Lance replied. "All previous participants are invited to join the last session each time the program is offered, it's a bit of a refresher. This session's speaker is particularly interesting. Organizations hire her to help them select the best and brightest when they have very senior positions to fill. Did you know we do that in our company?"

But before Ryan could respond, they were interrupted by a roaring round of applause as a tall woman with shoulder length, brown hair and wearing a red dress walked onto the stage.

"Well... Hello friends," she said. "Good to see some of you again... and for those who don't know me, I'm Mona and today we're going to explore the subject of neural pathways in the brain."

She paused for a few moments as everyone in the room quieted to pay attention to her.

"Let me start with a question. Stand up if you think what you learned in the training program will help you to consciously direct and shape the neural pathways in your brain."

A spotlight scanned the audience, stopping briefly on some of the people who were standing. Ryan was surprised to see the CEO of his company among them. Also standing was one of the vice-presidents of the National Railway Company and, standing at the table to the left of him was the Chief Human Resource Officer of the College he attended.

"Yes," Mona continued, "those of you who stood up are right. What you learned, if you implement it in your daily living, will help you to consciously direct and shape the neural pathways of your brain."

You spent most of your week learning about thoughts and how they affect your life, your relationships, your behaviour, and your emotions. In fact, you could say that your thoughts have become your blueprint for living. Every time we think something, or behave in a certain way, the neural pathway for that particular thought or behaviour gets stronger."

She paused again, and then continued. "Let me explain with an example, but I need a volunteer." The room was silent.

"Well... how about you?" she said pointing a finger in the direction of Ryan's table. Ryan nudged Lance. "Is she pointing at me?"

"Sure looks that way to me," he said.

Ryan could feel his face getting warm and his palms start to sweat. Lance prodded him.

"Come on, be a sport, stand up," he said.

The spotlight shifted from the speaker to Ryan, who slowly got to his feet."

Mona's voice softened. "May I ask your name?"

"It's Ryan, he replied meekly.

"Okay Ryan, let's do some Socratic teaching."

Ryan could feel his heart beating faster and faster Mona continued, her somewhat familiar voice had a calming, welcoming effect on him. At the same time, he found himself doing one, two, three, redirect to compose himself enough to focus on what she was saying.

"Tell me, Ryan, is there someone you know who, every time you see them, you feel upset, angry or anxious, even before you start to interact?"

Ryan immediately thought of his father-in-law.

"You don't have to tell me who it is," she added. "I just need you to think about your interactions with that person and be willing to share some of those interactions with us."

Speechless, Ryan hesitated and Lance nudged him again. "Come on, share with us Ryan. It will help us all."

Ryan still hesitated, momentarily considering if it might be possible to improve his relationship with his father-in-law. His sweating palms suggested he was going into autopilot mode. *'One, Two, Three, Redirect.'*

Finally, he plunged ahead. "Well, ever since I got married I've had a strained relationship with my father-in-law," he said.

"Can you tell me a little more about what makes it strained?" Mona asked.

"Well, it seems that whatever I say he disagrees, or he will come up with some alternative that he thinks is better or more current, as if he's trying to prove me wrong or embarrass me."

"So when you're having a conversation with him, do you think about him trying to one-up you, or embarrass you before the conversation begins, or during the conversation?"

"At this point I just expect it every time we're together. I know it will be like..." Ryan pondered a moment, "...like a competition of words with him. So before and during both, I guess."

"Okay," she went on, "so how do you respond when he does that?"

Ryan had to think about it for a moment. It occurred to him that he experienced a lot of Monkey Mind when he was with his father-in-law.

"Well, I get frustrated with him... and I guess I just try to restate my point... and explain why I hold the opinion I do. He, of course, will try to refute whatever I say again... so by the time I'm ready to leave I'm usually a bit resentful."

"Thank you Ryan," Mona said. "Now I am going to use your example to show how neural pathways are strengthened."

As Ryan sat down she continued. "The first time Ryan interacted with his father-in-law and his father-in-law did this verbal sparring, Ryan walked away feeling somewhat upset. So the interaction, talking with father-in-law, and the associated thoughts and emotions... frustration, feeling upset... were registered somewhere in Ryan's brain. Let's call that 'somewhere' a neural pathway.

"The second time Ryan interacted with his father-in-law, he again challenged Ryan to a duel of words and Ryan walked away from the interaction once again feeling upset and frustrated. The interaction again registered, but this time it registered in the same place as the first upsetting interaction, in the same neural pathway.

"The third time Ryan interacts with his father-in-law, again the same verbal warfare happens and this time Ryan walks away even more upset and more frustrated, even a bit angry. And where does this interaction register in Ryan's brain? Anyone?

The woman at Ryan's table responded: "In the same neural pathway as the first two interactions."

"Exactly… and every time the feelings of frustration and anger are registered in that particular neural pathway, which is associated with interacting with his father-in-law, that neural pathway is strengthened. In other words, the day comes when Ryan finds that just anticipating having a conversation with his father-in-law results in autopilot feelings of anger or frustration.

"Now isn't that exactly what you said Ryan? I asked you, when you're having a conversation with him if you think about him trying to one-up you, or embarrass you before the conversation begins or during the conversation. You said that you now just expect it every time you interact with him. You know it will be like a competition of words with him."

She paused a moment to let the audience digest what she had been saying, then went on.

"Think of a neural pathway like the first time you walk across the grass on your lawn. There is a slight visible remnant of where you walked. The second time you walk on the same path, the remnant becomes a bit more visible. As you continue to walk the same path the third and fourth and fifth times, what happens? Ryan?

"Of course the more times you walk on the same grass the clearer and more visible a path becomes."

"Right… And when the path becomes so entrenched or worn into the ground it is pretty obvious, then whenever you go to walk across your yard you automatically go to that exact same path. Remember, the path was once nonexistent, but over time it became firmly established in the grass and soil until now you just automatically go to that path. You're on autopilot!

"That's what happens in your brain. Every time you exhibit a certain behaviour or go to a certain way of thinking about something, or express a particular emotion in a certain situation, the path gets stronger until one day your brain automatically goes to that pathway. You don't even think about it anymore.

"So you see Ryan," she added as she refocused directly on him, "now, when you interact with your father-in-law you no longer consciously choose how you will respond to him. You simply go into autopilot mode… a kind of defend-your-position mode… not to mention that a similar type of neural pathway is being formed in his brain," she added as she looked at others in the room.

Ryan sat in silence pondering her explanation of why just being in his father-in-law's presence aggravated him. He stood up and addressed Mona.

"Excuse me… I have a question."

"Go ahead Ryan," she said.

"Is there a way to reverse that neural pathway? I mean, I get it now, why I always seem to be in a bad mood when my wife mentions that her father is coming to visit. But now that I know about this neural pathway, the bigger question for me is how I reverse it and get out of autopilot with him?"

"Excellent question," Mona replied. "Does anyone want to take a shot at it?"

The HR Director of the Medical Center stood up.

"I imagine that if neural pathways are strengthened by continuously doing the same thing over and over… then if we do something else, interrupt the autopilot behaviour by doing something different, then we can start a new neural pathway. So for Ryan, instead of doing the war of words thing, he would maybe do something else, like... I don't know, maybe change the topic, or do something that we talked about in the Dealing With Difficult People Session, just decide to be curious about why a person responds the way they do. Maybe Ryan can respond to his father-in-law with some curiosity, try to uncover why he holds a particular opinion, or why he feels the need to always challenge him... instead of going into defence mode or getting frustrated."

"Excellent," Mona responded.. "Thank you... Yes, imagine what would happen if Ryan decided to be curious about why his father-in-law responds the way he does. That would start a new neural pathway. And the more the new pathway is used, the stronger it will get, and the less the neural pathway of defence and frustration is used the weaker it will get.

"In fact, if you bring an attitude of curiosity to any situation or person you are in conflict with, you will find your thoughts moving away from anger and frustration to more non-judgmental thoughts.

"So to answer Ryan's question, yes. Not only can you weaken neural pathways but you can also create and strengthen the ones you want."

Another hand went up in the audience.

"Yes Anthony?"

"So then every time I activate one, two, three, redirect and force my mind back to the present, the neural pathway for focusing gets stronger?"

"Yes, exactly... very good. And remember, focusing strengthens the pathway that allows us to think through our words and actions, even when we are under stress. You might say that neurons that fire together wire together!"

Mona acknowledged another hand up across the room. Yes Les?"

"So what sort of things can we do on a daily basis to build our present moment awareness?"

"Another great question," she replied. "You can start by picking any one thing that you do every day. It could be brushing your teeth or washing dishes, or even drinking your morning coffee. And while you are doing that particular activity, force your mind muscle to focus solely on that activity. So if you're washing dishes, focus on the motion of scrubbing the pot, soaping the pot, the way the water feels on your hand while you're rinsing the pot, and so on. If your thoughts stray, take three breaths and redirect them to what you are doing. If you're a keener, do this with two or three things a day… the more the better. But remember there is no one recipe! What works for one person may not work for another. Sometimes you need to take the knowledge you've received here and create something that works just for you. We all have our own unique ways of reminding ourselves of what's important to us.

"Sometimes there are situations that have such a powerful hold on you that you need to precede or follow one, two, three, redirect with something else," she went on. "For some people, that something else is a key word that is meaningful to them. It could be something as simple as 'NEXT'… or a phrase. The phrase I often use is, "My thoughts can fuel my success or feed my failure. Some people have an ancient mantra they repeat.

"My friend has one of her daughter's hair ties and puts it around her wrist whenever she is going to visit her mother. She knows she sometimes goes into autopilot and reverts to adolescent behaviour when her mum criticizes her. So when she finds her thoughts drifting to where she doesn't want them to be, she gives the hair tie a little flick, which brings her back to the present moment. She follows that with one, two, three, redirect.

"Quite honestly," she added, "there are hundreds of creative ways you can interrupt your thoughts and redirect them to the present moment. If none of the more common ones work for you, create one that does. When I run this training program myself, I ask people to create something that they think will work for them. Recently, for example, someone came up with 'Change the Channel.' She said that if she doesn't like the thoughts in her mind, she will just change the channel.

"The idea came from the battle for who gets the TV remote in her house. When she has control of the remote she can change the channel to whatever she wants, and there are many channels to choose from. So, similarly, she is going to be the one to decide what she wants to listen to in her head. According to her, when you experience Monkey Mind, the monkey is in control of the remote.

"Another participant said he was a tactile person so he would interrupt his thought by always having a note pad with blank white sheets close by. When he finds his thoughts are not where he wants them to be, he interrupts them by taking out the note pad and just looking at it.

"I guess there's something about a blank page staring back at you, waiting for you to decide with the first pen stroke, what will go on that page. It empowers him to know that he has the power to fill that page with negativity, anger, disappointment, fear, or poetry, goals to achieve, productive work, or positive thoughts.

"I ran into him again a few weeks ago," she went on. "He said his morning ritual now is to spend a few minutes just looking at a crisp blank white sheet of paper to remind himself that he will be the one to determine what thoughts go on the blank paper."

As Mona was speaking, a man dressed in a white tuxedo approached the podium and handed her a black frame with what appeared to be a certificate of some sort. She thanked him, looked at the frame, and looked out at the audience.

"Well, it seems we have come to that time where we will now induct one of our participants into our ranks, and to do that I should present myself in my work uniform. Excuse me for a moment."

Mona left the stage and returned moments later, she had changed her clothes and it seemed her hair was a different colour. Ryan looked at the woman on the stage, turned to Lance in disbelief and exclaimed in a raised voice, "My God, it's Anaka!"

"Yes I know," Lance replied with a quiet chuckle.

Before he had a chance to process what was happening, he heard his name being called.

"Ryan, can you please come to the stage."

Ryan looked at Lance. "What's going on?" he asked, but only heard his name being called again. He slowly got up and walked to the stage with Lance following behind him. When they got there, Mona said nothing. She just smiled at Ryan, handed the microphone to Lance, and left.

"Ryan," he said, "it's my pleasure to offer you the position of Executive Director of Change Management. Congratulations!"

He handed Ryan the frame, Ryan still somewhat in shock, looked down at what it said:

There is a Giant Self inside all of us; a self where time stands still and only the present moment can be lived; a self where magic and reality can coexist in that one moment of all that was, is, and will be!